HE IS

An Advent study on the attributes of God

Published by Sacred Holidays. © 2018 Sacred Holidays

No part of this book may be reproduced or transmitted in any forms by any means, electronic or mechanical, including photocopying and recording, or by any information storage or retrieval system, except as may be expressly permitted by Sacred Holidays. Requests for permission should be sent to hello@sacredholidays.com. This does exclude sharing visuals of the study on social media—you are free to share what God is teaching you!

If you know someone who is unable to afford this study and you are unable to purchase it for him or her, please see the Discounts page under the Lent tab on www.sacredholidays.com or contact hello@sacredholidays.com for help. It is our desire to ensure that everyone is able to do this study and will not let cost be a barrier.

ISBN 978-1732850217

Unless otherwise noted, all Scripture quotations are from the ESV Study Bible
The Holy Bible, English Standard Version® (ESV®)
Copyright © 2001 Crossway, a publishing ministry of Good News Publishers
All rights reserved.
ESV® Permanent Text Edition* (2016)

Cover and interior design: Megan Sjuts | Building 07 (www.building07.com)
Edited by Molly Parker
Image from cover from Kara Whitten | @KailoChic | www.akailochiclife.com

To order additional copies of this resource:
Visit the online shop at www.sacredholidays.com/shop or contact us for bulk orders (over 50 studies) for special pricing and delivery at hello@sacredholidays.com.

Printed in the United States of America

Sacred Holidays, P.O. Box 131476, Spring, TX, 77381

Hello Friend!

Christmas season is finally here, and if I could use emoticons in this study, I'd have like four rows of heart-eye smiley faces with a few lit up Christmas trees sprinkled in between.

    This is my hope and prayer for you this year—that you would celebrate Him more than you ever have before, that you would know who **HE IS**.

    I promise to be honest with you throughout this study and not offer you fluffy words that hold little weight. Here's the first thing I'm gonna shoot to you straight—this will be hard. Actually, this will be really hard. Choosing to start a study during this time of year is a little crazy. The good news is, it's not impossible. The other good news is, you are with the right people—we love crazy at Sacred Holidays! We will come together and help cheerlead one another along through this study. We will not quit. We will not have another unfinished study on our shelves that shames us. No, this one we will finish and we will let the Lord mold us into His image as we study His Word and connect with Him and His story.

    Ready? Let's get started! **HE IS** worth celebrating!

Much love! Mean it.

Becky Kiser

@beckykiser | hello@sacredholidays.com
Founder + CEO of Sacred Holidays

P.S. Don't skip the intro sections. You will need 30 minutes to an hour to finish it, so mark off that time. You will be so glad you did. Promise.

P.P.S. To get the very most out of this study, be sure you are following us on all the things. Plus, we post resources daily that will encourage and equip you, as well as connect you with others.

Follow us on Instagram: @sacredholidays
Like us on Facebook: facebook.com/sacredholidays
Join our private Facebook Group, the Tribe: facebook.com/groups/SacredHolidaysTribe

And to make it easier for others and for us to find you, use #sacredholidays and tag @sacredholidays when you post about this study and what God is teaching you through it!

Table of Contents

HELLO FROM BECKY — 3

DO THIS BEFORE ADVENT BEGINS

HOW TO USE THIS STUDY — 10
REFLECT + COMMIT — 16

ADVENT CANDLE LIGHT WITH BECKY KISER

CANDLE 1: WHO DO YOU SAY HE IS? — 22
CANDLE 2: HE IS INVISIBLE (IMMATERIAL) — 26
CANDLE 3: HE IS MY LIGHT — 30
CANDLE 4: HE IS EVERYWHERE (OMNIPRESENT) — 34
CANDLE 5: HE IS HERE — 37

ADVENT STUDY DAYS

DAY 1: ALL-POWERFUL (OMNIPOTENCE) BY LISA WHITTLE — 42
DAY 2: SOVEREIGN BY ELIZABETH WOODSON — 46
DAY 3: JUST BY LEIGH KOHLER — 51
DAY 4: UNCHANGING (IMMUTABLE) BY DEANNA OPHEIM — 55
DAY 5: JEALOUS BY CHRISTINE HOOVER — 59
DAY 6: ETERNAL BY MARY WILEY — 64
DAY 7: HEALER BY MEGAN BURNS — 69
DAY 8: FAITHFUL BY JAMIE IVEY — 74
DAY 9: SURPASSING ORDINARY (TRANSCENDENT) BY ANDI ANDREW — 79
DAY 10: TRUTHFUL (VERACITY OF GOD) BY KATIE ORR — 83
DAY 11: COMFORTER BY SARAH MAE — 87
DAY 12: GOOD BY ASHLEY JACKSON — 92
DAY 13: RIGHTEOUS BY REMI ONAYEMI — 96

DAY 14: HOLY BY KAI A. PINEDA	**101**
DAY 15: ALL-KNOWING (OMNISCIENT) BY DEBRA PARKER	**106**
DAY 16: GRACIOUS BY ASHLEY IRONS	**110**
DAY 17: PROVIDER BY VIVIAN MABUNI	**115**
DAY 18: PROTECTOR BY TARA ROYER STEELE	**119**
DAY 19: MERCIFUL BY BROOKE SAXON-SPENCER	**123**
DAY 20: INFINITELY WISE BY LOGAN WOLFRAM	**127**

APPENDIX

FOR GROUPS AND GROUP LEADERS	**134**
ABOUT SACRED HOLIDAYS	**135**
CONTRIBUTORS + BIOS	**136**
10% FOR VULNERABLE WOMEN AND CHILDREN IN KENYA (LEARN MORE!)	**145**
EXCERPT FROM *SACRED HOLIDAYS: LESS CHAOS, MORE JESUS* BY BECKY KISER	**148**
LET'S REALLY STAY FRIENDS	**175**

Bonus

Read the first chapter of *Sacred Holidays: Less Chaos, More Jesus* by Becky Kiser!

HE IS

- ☐ **Candle 1:** Who Do You Say He Is?
- ☐ **Candle 2:** He is Invisible (Immaterial)
- ☐ **Candle 3:** He is My Light
- ☐ **Candle 4:** He is Everywhere (Omnipresent)
- ☐ **Candle 5:** He is Here

CHOOSE #LESSCHAOSMOREJESUS EACH DAY THIS ADVENT

- ☐ **Day 1:** All-Powerful *with Lisa Whittle*
- ☐ **Day 2:** Sovereign *with Elizabeth Woodson*
- ☐ **Day 3:** Just *with Leigh Kohler*
- ☐ **Day 4:** Unchanging *with Deanna Opheim*
- ☐ **Day 5:** Jealous *with Christine Hoover*
- ☐ **Day 6:** Eternal *with Mary Wiley*
- ☐ **Day 7:** Healer *with Megan Burns*
- ☐ **Day 8:** Faithful *with Jamie Ivey*
- ☐ **Day 9:** Surpassing Ordinary *with Andi Andrew*
- ☐ **Day 10:** Truthful *with Katie Orr*
- ☐ **Day 11:** Comforter *with Sarah Mae*
- ☐ **Day 12:** Good *with Ashley Jackson*
- ☐ **Day 13:** Righteous *with Remi Onayemi*
- ☐ **Day 14:** Holy *with Kai A. Pineda*
- ☐ **Day 15:** All-Knowing *with Debra Parker*
- ☐ **Day 16:** Gracious *with Ashley Irons*
- ☐ **Day 17:** Provider *with Vivian Mabuni*
- ☐ **Day 18:** Protector *with Tara Royer Steele*
- ☐ **Day 19:** Merciful *with Brooke Saxon-Spencer*
- ☐ **Day 20:** Infinitely *with Logan Wolfram*

SHARE THIS WITH OTHERS!
@SACREDHOLIDAYS | #SACREDHOLIDAYS

CUT ALONG THE DOTTED LINE + USE AS A BOOKMARK TO KEEP YOU ON TRACK THIS ADVENT

DO THIS BEFORE ADVENT BEGINS

HOW TO USE THIS STUDY

Hooray—the study is starting! I know it's pretty typical to skip intro sections, but take the time as you'll likely find this study a little different from what you've done before. Give yourself about 30 minutes to work through the entire intro of this study. However, at the end of that time, we can guarantee you will be ready for Advent!

For many of you, studying God's Word comes second nature, and for others, it can be overwhelming. Knowing how to study God's Word and walk with Him are lacking in our current culture. We tend to take what others have learned, letting social media, podcasts, church, and books become our crutch. These things aren't bad, but they can't be the only places we take in God's Word. So let's study His Word and celebrate who HE IS this Advent!

Now, let's chat about the study!

PICK YOUR PACE

We want you to choose your flow over the course of Advent. Traditionally Advent begins the four Sundays before Christmas and ends on Christmas day. You are welcome to follow that traditional schedule, or pick your own pace. We've given you 25 days of content: five light study days for when you light your Advent candles (typically on those Sundays) and 20 study days. You can start this on December 1st and go 25 straight days. Or you can start in November or halfway through December. There isn't a set way you have to do this study.

Trust the Spirit in you to lead you at your own pace, knowing that shame is not from your Father. I hate to put dates on study days because automatically our check-the-list selves take over. Enter with that come shame and failure when we don't meet our standards. Fight this. Connecting with Jesus is not a check-the-box thing; it's only a connecting with Jesus thing. Man created Bible studies and calendars and checkbox lists, so give yourself some grace. Deal?

ADVENT CANDLE LIGHTING & LIGHT FOCUSED SCRIPTURE STUDY

If you aren't familiar with Advent, the process of Advent candles will be a little strange for you, but it's something I highly encourage! It's a simple practice and will remind you throughout the day of what you are preparing your heart for. I recommend placing your candles where you will see them often. Have some at home, but also consider having some at work.

Using Advent candles is simple: just grab five candles and follow the prompts in the study. They can be any color, size, or style. I recommend using battery-operated candles if you have young children in the house or want to have candles at your place of work or dorm room.

Traditionally you light the first candle the fourth Sunday before Christmas and then one more each subsequent Sunday, lighting the final one on Christmas day. However, follow your own plan if you'd rather. We put these days at the beginning of the study so you can plug it in when you want. If you aren't familiar with this process, I recommend setting out a note on Sundays to remind yourself about it and make it a priority. Then simply follow the prompts and let your heart engage with Scripture on those days.

- **Where could you put your Advent candles so you see them often?**

Keep it simple. You will need five candles, and they can be any size and any color.

- **What supplies do you need? When can you get them? Mark your calendar.**

For more information about Advent candles, watch the following videos on the Sacred Holidays YouTube channel:

https://www.youtube.com/watch?v=_hLei2SnJGI

https://www.youtube.com/watch?v=-n5FEZrItcc

PRAYER PROMPT TO START EACH SESSION

Every day we start with prayer because learning to talk to our Father is a hard discipline. Fight the temptation to skip this prompt. I use the acronym PRAY and then pause to Wait and Listen.

PRAISE: Thank God for who He is and what He has done—in His Word and all around you.

REPENT: Confess sin—the things that separate us from Him.

ASK: Request things for others, for things going on in the world, or whatever else He brings to mind.

YIELD: Surrender yourself and anything going on in your life today to your Father.

WAIT AND LISTEN: Pause afterwards and listen to see if God speaks back to you. You won't likely hear an audible voice (I never have), but you will experience a knowing. The more you listen the more you will hear that voice in your heart, as the Holy Spirit speaks. And oftentimes we get our response the next time we open His Word!

You might prefer to grab a journal to write out prayers if you need more space. Or you can pray without writing. I do a little bit of both—I jot down key words and then talk to the Father.

DOER OF THE WORD APPLICATION

We can often rush off at the end of time spent in Bible study. When we do this, we keep the knowledge of what we've learned in our heads and even our hearts, but don't let it go to our hands, mouths, or feet. Let's change that this year! After we have studied His Word, let's live out the command found in James 1:22, "Do not merely listen to the Word, and so deceive yourselves. Do what it says . . ."

At the end of each day you will see this prompt:

> **DOER OF THE WORD**
>
> How can you apply what you have learned from the Lord today?

This prompt is really centered on taking action on a truth you read about that day and applying it to your own life. The Lord might challenge you to respond somehow, like waking up earlier to get in His Word or pray with more faith. He might correct you, asking you to stop doing something, like gossiping or judging a certain person or group.

There might be some days you have several things you need to do, and other days this stays blank—both are totally fine! The important thing is that you pause and ask the Lord if there is anything you should do.

SOCIAL CHALLENGE

While the What Should I Do application gets us thinking about areas we need to change in our lives, the Who Should I Tell challenge focuses more on sharing with others what God is teaching you. Don't worry, we aren't going to have you go knock on strangers' doors every day, or even any day for that matter. The intent is way more natural. After you've talked to your Father in prayer, studied His Word, become a doer of His Word, you are ready to tell others! Jesus's final command was to go and make disciples (Matthew 28). Because we love others, we should want to share what is true with them!

The problem is, this often makes us very uncomfortable. We don't want to offend, so we say nothing at all. We fear that sharing something others might not agree with is unloving, so we choose silence instead. Hear me, this is not the best way we can love them. If we really believe what God is teaching us is true, than we should share it with others.

Some days you will have something to tell, other days you won't. The point is that you slow down and ask the Father to give you a courageous heart and brave feet. You can do this!

// **WHAT IS SOMETHING YOU CAN SHARE ABOUT TODAY?**

// **STOP AND ASK GOD TO SHOW YOU WHO TO SHARE THIS WITH TODAY.**

// **WHO SHOULD YOU SHARE THIS WITH? (FINISH SENTENCE BELOW.)**

THIS MESSAGE IS *FOR ALL* BUT IT IS ALSO FOR:

// **PRAY OVER THAT PERSON(S) OR GROUP AND ASK GOD FOR AN OPPORTUNITY AND COURAGE TO SHARE.**

IF YOU SHARE ON SOCIAL MEDIA
BE SURE TO USE #SACREDHOLIDAYS + TAG @SACREDHOLIDAYS.

People or groups to consider when deciding who to tell each day:

- People you live with (i.e., family or roommates)
- Co-workers
- Extended family members
- Friends
- Neighbors
- Strangers (look up when you are out and about)
- Social Media friends and followers

We have so many ways we can tell people: in person, text, phone call, email, or whatever way you communicate. You can also share more broadly by posting on social media. During seasons like Christmas, many are more open to hearing these kinds of truths. We know this is true because churches are packed on Christmas. They want to be a part of this story, many just don't know how to find their way to it. You can help by telling them what is true about the Father.

"Go therefore and make disciples of all nations, baptizing them in the name of the Father and of the Son and of the Holy Spirit, teaching them to observe all that I have commanded you. And behold, I am with you always, to the end of the age."

Matthew 28:19-20

STAY CONNECTED

Research shows that when you do something with others, you are more likely to follow through and have better results. It's the reason why Weight Watchers, CrossFit, and all our friends online want us to join their fitness groups for just 30 days—when you do things with others, you are more likely to succeed.

You don't have to do this study alone! I love doing studies with other people for two main reasons: it forces me to stick with it, and I love learning what they have learned. Inevitably, when we start talking, someone will share something I didn't even see. Or their faith encourages me to push into Jesus more, instead of going after Him half-heartedly.

Here are a few ways you can stay connected with others:

1| Join the Sacred Holidays Tribe (our private Facebook group). This is a great space to go when you want to connect with others who want the same thing out of Advent as you do. There, you can share what God has taught you that day, share prayer requests (we love messy and vulnerable), and be accepted just as you are.

☐ **Go to facebook.com/groups/SacredHolidaysTribe to join and then check the box next to this prompt.**

2| Ask a few friends to join you! It's never too late because with Amazon Prime, this study can be in your friends' hands in just two days (and for free shipping, too!). Plus, doing this with others is not just so much more fun, but it is so much more beneficial—for them and you! We know life is crazy-busy right now, but you have space and time for this and will not regret the value it brings.

- *Who are 2-5 friends you could text right now and ask to join you?*

3| Host or co-host a group—we give you all you need to lead! If you are interested in hosting a group—online or in person, small or big—check-out our Group page on the Sacred Holidays website. Also, we have a private Facebook Group just for our Group leaders to share tips, prayer requests, and encouragement.

If you don't want to host a group, but you'd love to be in a group, check out our Group page at sacredholidays.com/join-a-group to see if there is one in an area near you.

REFLECT + COMMIT

Now, let's be realistic. To really do this and do it well, we want to go in strong and prepared. Take the time to complete the reflection and commitment section below.

REFLECT

- **What have been some of your biggest regrets from past Advent/Christmas seasons?**

- **Why did you decide to do this Advent study?**

- **How would you describe your relationship with the Lord right now? Be honest.**

- **How often do you spend focused time with Him—not rushed or on-the-go time, but still and focused time with Him (some call this a "quiet time")? What do you do during this time?**

- **What does studying the Word of God look like for you in this current season?**

- *What does prayer look like for you in this current season?*

- *What do you hope to get out of this study and season?*

COMMIT

Do you know that most women struggle to spend time with God? They do. Studying God's Word takes effort; it doesn't come easily or naturally. So if you feel frustrated that you are always behind on studies (and you know we don't believe in behind) or feel shame that you never stick with studies, let us help you!

Start with grace. Because He offers it to you freely, give yourself grace and pick up where you left off. If you feel overwhelmed by the study or the season, give yourself grace . . . again (and reach out to us, so we can help you).

- *Write below: "I will give myself grace."*

With that said, be disciplined. Giving yourself grace is not the same thing as being lazy. You can do this. This may feel hard at times and it will certainly be a challenge, but you've done harder.

- *Write down three things you've done that are harder than finishing a Bible study:*

    1.

    2.

    3.

- *Write below: "I will not quit."*

One thing I've realized about myself is how many little obstacles I let take up my time throughout the day. When I choose to be more disciplined in those areas, it creates more time than I realize.

- **When will you choose to have time with the Lord each day? Pick a time and a place.**

- **Set an alarm on your phone each day, setting it 10 minutes before you're ready to meet with God. Turn on the snooze feature so you can hit snooze until you actually get started. Initial below when you've set your alarm.**

- **What obstacles might prevent you from making this time a reality? I want you to think about what distracts you once you're about to sit down or have already sat down. List each one below. Then write down what you can do to eliminate or lessen each distraction. (For example, I know that if I even pick up my phone in the morning I will get lost in the rabbit hole that is Instagram for 20 minutes. So I don't allow myself to touch it until I've spent time with the Lord.)**

OBSTACLES	WHAT CAN YOU DO ABOUT IT?

- *Write a prayer to the Lord committing this study to Him. Ask Him to help you. Ask Him to move in your heart and life during this Lent season. (You can write your prayer on the inside cover of your study.)*

- *Share your chart with someone, or with several people, and write their names below. Give them full permission to ask you how you are doing and help hold you accountable to the goals you've set.*

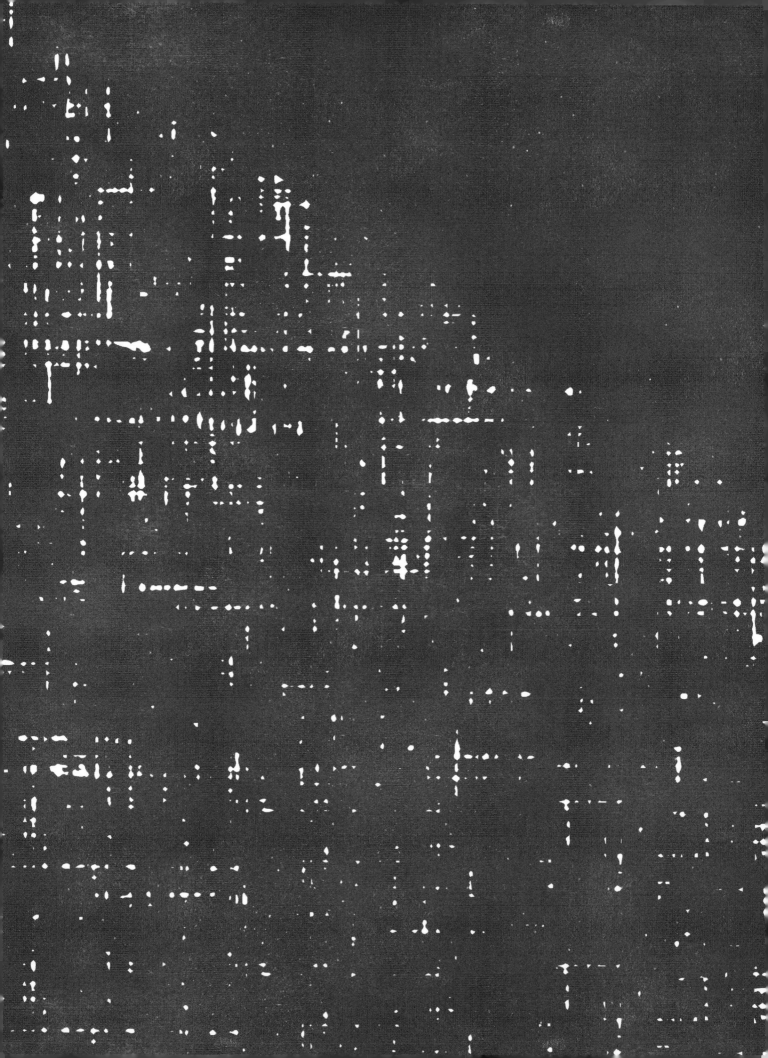

ADVENT
CANDLE DAYS

Who Do You Say He Is?

I can't believe the Christmas season is actually here! You are done with all things fall-colored and flavored (except pumpkin spice, we will never be done with pumpkin spice), and it is now completely acceptable to display Christmas decorations without the judgment of your neighbors.

Transitioning between all the chaos of the holidays can be tricky. One of the best ways to help pursue #LessChaosMoreJesus is to give the transition some reflection.

- ☐ **If you haven't already filled out the Reflect + Commit section, go back to that now. You won't regret those extra 10 minutes. Promise.**

- ☐ **Now is also a good time to pull-out or order your copy of Sacred Holidays: Less Chaos, More Jesus to plan out what other things—holy and set apart—you want to pursue this coming Advent season. If you don't yet have your copy, you can order it anywhere books are sold online or grab a copy in Lifeway bookstores.**

This year will be different because you chose to show up here. I'm so proud of you. Our hope is that you experience life-change as you see God for all He is, giving you a new awareness that changes the way you love Him, yourself, and others.

Oh I'm giddy for you, and I also wish you were sitting across from me in the booth that is my writing spot today. You'd laugh at me because it's in the bar section at my favorite restaurant to get work done—not your typical Bible study writing location, ha! I'm sipping steaming French press coffee and iced tea (because I'm apparently a caffeine addict) with my laptop up, planner laid open, and Bible spread out. Though if you were with me, I would shut those things down and look you in the eyes so you could see the sincerity in my words: I love you, and I'm so very excited you are here. I've been praying for you long before you held these pages. We are constantly asking God to let the words on these pages—and the space you make for this time to actually happen—be a clear way for you to hear from your Father. One thing I love about Bible studies is we often hear something from God that maybe we just couldn't get on our own. Or maybe we are getting it on our own, and the Lord is relentless in confirming it again, and again, and again.

This study is all about the attributes, or characteristics, of God. We are going to be looking at what the Word of God says He is, and then celebrate who He is this Advent! But before we do, we need to establish a starting point for who we already believe He is.

Who do you say He is? Describe God with five attributes:

(Note: it's tempting to answer using our best Christian-ese. Fight that tendency, and get vulnerable and honest. Today, with all your joy and pain, in your current circumstances, who is God to you or who has He been in the past?)

1. Sovereign → Knows Best
2. Shepherd → Leads me beside still waters
3. Safe Place ~ Grace, Compassion, Patience
4. Stable - Not hype → I AM
5. Storm Calmer → Quiet me with your Love

- **Read Mark 8:27-30 and write out the questions Jesus asked:**

"Who do you say that I am?"

When I'm reading Scripture, there are so many times I wish I could be there to get the tone and the full context. I wish I could see the look in Jesus's eyes so I could try to discern His intent with each question. One thing I know is that He asked who the people said He was, before asking who Peter said He was.

We can be certain He cares about each one of us individually.

We can also be certain we cannot hide behind the opinions and beliefs of others. We must, alone, answer the question. You are not your church home. You are not your parents. You are not your roommates, or your spouse, or your best friends. You, alone, matter to God. Your faith, alone, matters. Your answering alone means something to Jesus.

The beautiful thing about God is that the pressure is off. Our good deeds and our right answers aren't needed—just our heart, our lives surrendered to Him. When we aren't sure what to believe, or feel trapped in sin or suffocated by insecurity, there is One who is coming to enlighten our present reality.

- **Read John 1:4-5, 9 and write what is used to describe Jesus.**

Life-giving, Light, Overcomer,

One of my favorite things about Christmas is the lights. They feel magical. When I started celebrating Advent, using candles to celebrate what was coming, my whole focus was constantly being shifted. The first things I do when I wake up are plug in my tree and light my candles. (Actually, I turn on the battery candles because I have three young kiddos and fire isn't a good idea, ha!) Those candles remind me of the One my heart should focus on. I pass those candles so often during my day, and it's not a one-moment game changer, but a "small moment by small moment" attention shifter. Those five candles now bring all the whimsy of the sparkly tree they sit next to, for they remind me how desperately I need the light of Christ in my life. I need God to be light because life, even when it's good, still feels dark.

- **How does life feel dark for you? Or how do you feel in the dark?**

Lost in purpose - Not handling life well with Productivity & Relationships

LIGHT YOUR FIRST ADVENT CANDLE.

(Note: See the intro section for more details on Advent candle lighting.)

My friend, God is light. It is His coming, His light to your darkness, that you are celebrating this Christmas! As we read about who He is each day, your world will brighten. Life may not get easier, and that's fine; easier isn't our aim. Knowing Him is our aim. Focusing on His light is our aim.

We started today by saying who we believe God to be, and we are going to wrap up today hearing about who He says *we are*.

- **Read 1 Peter 2:9 and write the four things God says you are.**

1. Chosen People
2. Royal Priesthood
3. Holy Nation
4. God's Special Possession

Those words sound nice, but the meaning of them can get lost on us. I wish I was a Greek expert and could properly dissect them for you, but I'm not. Thankfully we don't need a fancy degree to be able to interpret the Word of God. We have the Spirit who is our Helper. Jesus said that "the Helper, the Holy Spirit . . . <u>will teach you all things</u>" (John 14:26).

- ***Wrap up today by asking your Helper, the Holy Spirit, to show you the meaning for each of these names your Father, the True Light, has called you:***

I am a "Chosen Race":

I am a "Royal Priesthood":

I am a "Holy Nation":

I am a "People for His Own Possession":

Oh sister, He loves you, He chose you, He calls you royal, He sees you as holy, and you better believe He wants you for His own.

- ***Do you know why He wants you all for His own? Write out the second part of 1 Peter 2:9.***

To Declare the praises of Him who called you out of darkness

As you focus on who God's Word says He is this Advent season, I'm praying that you will feel Him bringing you out of darkness and into light, "His marvelous light."

He Is Invisible (Immaterial)

Some of these attributes, okay let's be honest, all of these can feel impossible to wrap our minds around. *You know what? We don't have to wrap our minds around them, just our faith.* Ask God to give you the faith to believe He is all He says He is, He has done all we've read about, and He can do all He says He will do.

One of the hardest things for me about believing and following God is that I can't see Him. Faith has never come easily or naturally for me. I am a natural skeptic, so faith has been something I've had to fight for, even now nearly two decades after first choosing to follow Jesus.

- **Do you struggle with faith in a God you can't see or is it something that comes naturally to you? How so?**

> Naturally - Grew up with parents who spoke of Him often - as if He was in the room.

His Word has been life to me because it has revealed who *He Is*. His Word speaks into and is able to contain all my fears and questions. When I struggle with just wanting a burning bush moment where God makes Himself so clear, I find great comfort when I read in His Word that He is invisible. 1 Timothy 1:17 says, "Now to the King eternal, immortal, invisible, the only God, be honor and glory forever." 1 Timothy 6:16 says, ". . . whom no one has seen or can see." John 1:18 says, "No one has ever seen God."

But His Word also says in Romans 1:20: "For since the creation of the world God's invisible qualities, his eternal power and divine nature, have been clearly seen, being understood from what has been made, so that men are without excuse." And in Colossians 1:15, "He [Jesus] is the image of the invisible God…"

I love how God acknowledges we can't see Him, yet He doesn't leave us in the dark; He sends us the Light, Jesus, the image of the invisible God. This is what this Christmas season is all about—setting our blind eyes on the invisible God who was made visible through His Son.

- **Read Isaiah 42:16 and write out the "I will" statements of God.**

Friend, did you need to hear all those things He says He will do for you? I know I did! There is so much unknown in our lives, and it can be frustrating, terrifying, annoying, or heartbreaking. Sometimes our unknowns can seem so insignificant that we are irritated by how much they irritate us.

- *What are some unknowns you face?*

  Health, girls leaving, parents' health

- *How do they make you feel?*

  Anxious, afraid, lost

- *How do they make you feel about God?*

  God will be with me but He makes no promises to make life easy. That makes me sad — I wish His children would have an easier life...

We all have unknowns—significant or seemingly insignificant. As hard as the not-knowing is for me, knowing that God *knows* brings me a significant amount of comfort. Not in a fake smile, "I'm blessed" kind of a way; those people aren't fooling anyone but themselves. Nope. Rather, God's way of knowing brings this indescribable, resolute confidence that it's all going to be okay because of who He is.

- *Look back at that passage and note what God tell us He will do with darkness.*

LIGHT YOUR SECOND ADVENT CANDLE.

(Note: See the intro section for more details on Advent candle lighting.)

He says He will lead us in ways we could never fathom, down roads we never knew about. As He does all of those things, the darkness changes to light.

I love this stage of Advent, when only two of our candles are lit, because it so perfectly represents not all is dark and not all is light. We are on that path towards light. We are in the unknown still. We can see some, but not fully.

If you are in Christ, you have not been overcome by the dark and unknown that surrounds you. Do not live in defeat my friend. It is not yours to own. Romans 8:37 says, "We are more than conquerors"—not just dominators, but we dominate dominating because of "him who loved us."

So whatever unknown is before you, know today that it will not overcome you. More than that, it is actually good for you. I want you more than anything to see the goodness of God in the unknown that causes so many aches. He is for you. I can prove it.

- **Read James 1:2-4 and write out the ripple effect of trials.**

The unknown can feel like God is withholding from us, but in reality, He doesn't want us to be without or lacking anything. The hard of the unknown is that it's for our good, that we may be *"perfect and complete."*

- **Do you feel perfect and complete yet? Why or why not?**

No ~ not until heaven

If not, that's okay (and by the way, I'm guessing most of us answered "not yet"). Go back on the ripple effect of trials. Are you being steadfast? No? The problem could lie there, not in what God is or isn't doing. Being steadfast simply means that you are focused and aren't easily distracted.

- **Would you consider yourself steadfast? Why?**

- **What would steadfast look like for you? How can you make that happen?**

It's okay for God to test your faith. It's not fun or awesome, but it's good. Sometimes we need to be reminded that we are blind—we don't know what's going on. In these reality checks we can experience our God who says, "I will turn darkness before them into light, the rough places into level ground. These are the things that I will do, and I do not forsake them" (Isaiah 42:16b).

He is My Light

Hello, friend! You are halfway through Advent!

- **How has focusing on who He Is affected your heart this Christmas? Journal your thoughts below. Also, ask the Father to reveal anything you need to surrender so you may worship Him more fully and freely.**

One of my very best friend's home caught on fire last week. So much is gone. It has been one thing after another for her and her family—years of infertility with three babies lost and now this too. Some things just don't seem fair. Even so, though they've lost their home and many things in it, their faith hasn't been shaken. They can't even explain how they are okay with all that is happening, but they are okay.

Friend, this can only happen when we take our eyes off of what is happening (or not happening) around us and set our gaze on the One we are waiting for this Christmas—Jesus.

- **Read all of Psalm 27, out loud if possible, and note anything that is said of the Lord.**

He doesn't just provide the light; He is the Light (Psalm 27:1)!

- **Read John 8:12 and write it below.**

LIGHT YOUR THIRD ADVENT CANDLE.

(Note: See the intro section for more details on Advent candle lighting.)

- ***What does verse 12 say about our part in being in the light?***

We have to follow Jesus. That's it. Simple enough, right? Ha! It's so hard. I hate that it's hard. I don't want it to be hard. I feel foolish that it's hard, but it is hard to follow Jesus. I mean, not really hard, because there are things in life that are actually hard (like fighting cancer, going through a divorce, being without a job, children starving, unending loneliness, etc). Regardless, for most of us, following Jesus is a struggle.

- ***Does following Jesus feel like a struggle most days for you?***

I think most of us overcomplicate following Jesus. In our overachieving society, we think we need to do more. In our social media society, we have visuals to prove that we aren't following Jesus right . . . or at least not as awesome as her. Truth? There isn't a magical formula to following Jesus. Following Jesus is simply choosing to actually follow Him. This following looks different for each person because we are all different.

If you want to follow someone, what do you do? You focus on them and do whatever they show you. You listen intently to whatever they say. You don't take your eyes off of them. It involves a lot of trust and even more effort. It won't just happen.

We watched the Olympics this summer, and one event that leaves me in total awe is synchronized diving. I have no clue how they do it. First, how do they stay in sync like that? Second, how do they stay in sync being different heights and weights? I'm so not a science girl, but I remember there are big words that describe how things fall at different speeds because of size and other factors. So how in the world do these people, who are totally different in nature, stay completely in sync while they are jumping, twisting, flipping, turning, and arching, before crashing into the water?! It's insane.

- ***How do you think they do it?***

I'm sure your answer had something to do with lots of practice and probably something to do with working with their partner. I would guess those are right answers. Those Olympians didn't take up diving last week. It took years and years of practice and meets, lots of failures, and plenty of injuries—and they never quit. They put on that suit and did it again and again . . . and again. The mundane, routine, boring, and insignificant led them to that diving board, with the eyes of the world watching, all while having a partner to consider. They had to work closely, learning more about their partner than they know about themselves. There is a unity off the board long before they step onto the board. Distractions must become obsolete and the goal of unity preeminent.

- ***What often distracts your gaze from Jesus and walking with Him?***

When we choose to follow Him (not others, and not our own ways), we invite light into our lives. The darkness dissipates as we enter into the light. The same happens as we now have three candles lit instead of just two. Slowly, but surely, things are getting lighter as we focus more and more on the One who is coming!

Remember my friends whose house caught on fire? They keep sharing one unbelievable story of God's provision after another. They aren't focused on the countless surgeries, medicines, appointments, and babies lost. Instead they are focused on the legacy of those babies and the infertility ministry that has been birthed through their suffering. Their gaze isn't on what is covered in literal ashes, it's on the God who had them out of the house that night, with their two little miracle boys safe! They aren't faking a bubbly joy. They aren't pretending all is awesome, because it's not. However, when they focus on all God has done and is doing, there is so much peace.

Life from death. Beauty from ashes.

- ***Read Psalm 27 one more time and write out verse 8 as a commitment.***

- ***Knowing God is your light, how can you make more of an effort to seek His face?***

- *Is there a person or group you can share this with, a group that'll encourage you to seek God? Write their name(s) below and put a check next to each name after you've reached out to them.*

I am praying for you often, my friend. If you ever need someone on our team to pray for you specifically, email us at hello@sacredholidays.com or PM/DM us on social media (@sacreholdiays).

He is Everywhere (Omnipresent)

I know you probably have very little time this week, so let's not waste another a minute. Let's dig right into the truth that is life and light this Advent. Fight for this time and this space. Everything else is secondary to this sacred time. Choose dry shampoo instead of a fancy, blown-out style if that's what it takes (which is me about 95% of the time). Choose waking up early (ugh, I know) if that's the only way it'll work with this week's schedule. This isn't something you have to do, but oh, life will be more full and free when you go before Him.

The beauty of our God is that He isn't hiding or holding out on us.

- **Record what you learn about God from Psalm 139:7-12.**

There isn't a place you could go where He isn't already there, turning darkness to light.

- **What are some places where you specifically feel like God is present and His light shining?**

For me, it is outdoors. If I can find myself outside, or by an awesome window, then my faith begins to soar again. The things in my life that feel dark or unknown begin to lighten when I'm surrounded by nature; it is there I more clearly see Him everywhere. I love how Romans 1:20 says it: "For since the creation of the world God's invisible qualities—his eternal power and divine nature—have been clearly seen, being understood from what has been made, so that people are without excuse."

- **Read Ephesians 5:8-10 and write what it tells us to do in response to God's light.**

Our job is pretty simple: "Live as children of the light." It's actually not simple because we are human, and He is God. However, we can make every effort to walk as He did, to not just see and worship His light, but to also follow His light.

Answer the questions as honestly as you can. In the first column you will see a topic and questions. Go ahead and answer in the second column how you "walk" in those areas. Then in the third column, pause and pray to ask God how you could better imitate Him (repent if you need to). We want to go through

QUESTIONS	HOW DO I WALK?	IMITATE GOD
SPEECH: Do you gossip? Lie? Speak negatively? Encourage?		
SIGHTS & SOUNDS: What do you expose your eyes and ears to? TV and movies? Music?		
COMMUNITY: Do you let people see the good and the ugly? Make every effort to love the community around you?		
OUTREACH: Are you stuck in a Christian bubble? Do you know lost people? Do you serve people willingly and often?		
HEALTH & WELLNESS: How do you take care of yourself? How is your physical body? Your purity? Food intake?		
CAREER & PASSION: Do you seek Him for the next steps in your career? Are you brave to do what He gives you? Do you love your co-workers well?		
FINANCES: Are you in debt? Budgeting well? Controlling the desire for greed? Blessing others with what you do have?		
TIME WITH THE LORD: How often do you spend time with Jesus? Do you long for it or dread it? Apply it or just check the box?		
(You can add something)		

every aspect of our lives and really ask ourselves, "How do I walk?" Is it as a child of light or another way? Be specific. Don't rush, but reflect and ask God to show you what walking in His light—His light that is everywhere—looks like in each context.

- ***Wrap-up today by writing down a prayer to God, thanking Him for being everywhere and asking Him to help you be a light for Him everywhere you go.***

LIGHT YOUR FOURTH ADVENT CANDLE.

(Note: See the intro section for more details on Advent candle lighting.)

Now that your fourth candle is lit, I send you out with this: "The Lord is near to all who call on Him, to all who call on Him in truth" (Psalm 145:18).

This Christmas is different because you are different. You are a child of the Light. You are walking in the Light. Yes, you can still blast the holiday songs, binge on Hallmark movies, go crazy getting gifts, eat way too many sweets, and turn your home into Santa's Wonderland. However, this time your Christmas won't be wrapped up with all that. There won't be a "so this is all?" feeling after the last gift is opened because it's not over; you are just getting started.

God is everywhere, and He has called you to walk in the Light and shine it everywhere you go.

He is Here

Merry Christmas! He is here, friend! I know this day is full, so I'm super proud of you for sneaking away for some time with your Father. I'm not going to make today light just because it's Christmas (#sorrynotsorry). In fact the opposite is true; I want you to have so much of Him today. So you might need to do a little, and then come back later to wrap-up—whatever works for you to celebrate and soak Him up.

LIGHT YOUR FIFTH, AND FINAL, ADVENT CANDLE.

(Note: See the intro section for more details on Advent candle lighting.)

- ***Read James 1:17 and write it below.***

I'm not sure what Christmas is like for you—if it's flooded with gifts, or if you long for the piles of gifts. Regardless of what your day brings, I know this for certain: everything comes from your Father of Lights—everything that is good and everything that is perfect.

- ***Stop for a moment and list out everything you can think of in your life that is good or perfect. (Do this for five minutes.)***

Today is all about celebrating His presence—Jesus has come! At the risk of sounding cheesy I must add, the very greatest and most perfect gift your Father of Lights has given you was Jesus, born of a virgin and placed in a manger.

- **The Christmas Story is long, but worth your time. Read all of Luke 1:26-55 and 2:1-21, and note all the significant parts of the story.**

Imagine you are Joseph or Mary. And imagine being told what the angel Gabriel told them. I struggle putting myself in their shoes. Things so did not go the way they had imagined!

- **Has God ever totally changed your plans in a drastic way? How so?**

Gabriel knew that the baby growing within the Virgin Mary's belly was Jesus, God in flesh, who is all-powerful, sovereign, just, unchanging, and jealous.

Moving a few weeks into her pregnancy, I wish I could've seen the reunion between Mary and Elizabeth. Isn't it the best to have someone get and accept your crazy?! I imagine so many people questioned Mary and the truth of her story, which brought her to someone who would love, trust, and rejoice in what God had done, as crazy as it may have seemed.

- **Do you have someone like this? Recall a time when you've shared your crazy and been fully accepted.**

The God Mary bragged about to Elizabeth is the same One we have studied. He is eternal, healer, faithful, surpassing ordinary, and truthful. How beautiful to have a God who is all of those things yet still gives the good gift of people—who accept us for who we are, right where we are.

I can't even pretend to put myself in Mary's place: nine-and-a-half months pregnant, just having ridden a donkey a long way, only to find out there is nowhere to stay! I would've lost my mind, and likely lost it on someone! She gave birth to Jesus right outside the inn because there wasn't room for them. God worked a miracle even though there wasn't a typical place for her.

- **Do you feel like there isn't a place for you, that all the "rooms" are filled, and you and your gifts aren't needed?**

This is a lie. Your Father of Lights, who gives good gifts, is comforter, good, righteous, holy, and all-knowing. He has a place for you, it just might not look like what you imagine. However, the space doesn't affect the significance.

Finally, angels fill the sky above the shepherds out in a field to tell them Christ has been born! I love how God doesn't consider our ranking in life. He isn't impressed with the popularity others attribute to us. He told the shepherds first about His Son, Jesus, being born! The shepherds, whose ranking socially wasn't awesome, are who God chose to tell first.

- **Do you feel like you still aren't at the popular table? Even though you are an adult, do you struggle with feeling significant?**

You are significant. And if I had to guess, if you answered yes to the first question, then you are right where God wants you. He loves working with the unlikely; it gives Him more to show off with because our God is gracious, provider, protector, merciful, and infinitely wise. He has an affinity for doing crazy amazing things with people we least suspect. It's one of my favorite parts about Him.

- **Wrap-up today by writing out James 1:17 again, and thank your Father for His gift of coming and all He has done this Advent season.**

ADVENT STUDY DAYS

ALL-POWERFUL (OMNIPOTENCE)
by Lisa Whittle

PRAISE GOD. REPENT OF SIN. ASK FOR OTHERS + YOURSELF.

YIELD TO GOD TODAY. WAIT + LISTEN.

In this beautiful season, Jesus's followers hold some treasured gifts: His Spirit, alive and in us; a personal Savior, caring about the deepest needs of our heart; Almighty God, our Father who is powerful, steady, and strong. Jesus came into this world by the very power of God, and it is this unbreakable thread of His nature that continues to hold this world together. Clinging to verses like Jeremiah 32:17 is a lifeline for every weary believer's soul: "O Sovereign Lord! You have made the heavens and earth by Your great power. Nothing is too hard for You!" But here's the rub—being human is to live in this world's mess and yet have eyes only on God's infinite power.

- *Read Luke 1:35. Imagine you received such news. How would you react?*

   Disbelief? Did that happen?

Jesus's own mother at first struggled to grasp how such a miracle could occur inside of her. And still today, Jesus knows we need reminders that God is with us, for us, and has us, no matter the particular life storm we face. We need His miraculous power to get us up in the morning, keep us alive with hope, and move us toward the thriving life. Only an omnipotent God could do such compelling things.

- *Whether you've seen God's power displayed through a healed sickness, a restored family, or faithful provision, describe a time you've witnessed His omnipotence.*

   ~ My spirit still loves Jesus - through hard times - that's God's grace

Consider the following four aspects of God's power:

He is powerful in us. One of the most beautiful aspects of the power of God is that He does not keep it only for Himself, but offers it liberally to those of us who trust in Him. Ephesians 3:20 says, "Now to Him who is able to do above and beyond all that we ask or think, according to the power that works in us." God working in and through us are gifts which allow His children to share in the Kingdom work, and He takes great pleasure in seeing this put to action. As we see in 2 Peter 1:3—"By his divine power, God has given us everything we need for living a godly life"—the Father willfully chooses to show the world how weakness can be made perfect by supernatural strength. When we operate in God's full strength, we show the world the manifestation of His power.

He is powerful with us. Jesus was powerfully with Moses when He led the Israelites in their harrowing escape from Egypt and in the difficulties of the barren wilderness. He was powerfully with Esther when she approached the king to save her people from death. This same God is equally as powerful with us today, in our daily lives, complications, and deep desert moments. Our job is to remember His power and call on His help. Ephesians 1:19-20 attests to this: "I pray that you will begin to understand the incredible greatness of his power for us who believe him. This is the same mighty power that raised Christ from the dead and seated Him in the place of honor at God's right hand in the heavenly realms."

He is powerful for us. Perhaps the most blessed assurance Jesus followers have is that God is on our side. We see it in Romans 8:31: "If God is for us, who can be against us?" God is for us. He is powerful on our behalf. The battles we fight are not ours. The enemy we face has to face Him. This understanding changes our security in life and like David, draws us to the loving face of God: "When I look at the night sky and see the work of Your fingers—the moon and the stars You have set in place—what are mortals that You should think of us, mere humans that You should care for us?" (Psalm 8:3-4)

He is powerful despite us. I'm so thankful that God's power is not contingent upon our ability to feel or be strong. That He works outside the realm of human limitation is among the greatest gifts to His creation. Never will anyone match the power of God. Never will anyone even come close. This is the God we follow and live for, and may this knowledge seep deep and strengthen our hearts. "Now he is far above any ruler or authority or power or leader or anything else in this world or in the world to come" (Ephesians 1:21 NLT).

- **Which of the previous aspects of God's power speaks loudest to you?**

Powerful For Us → Jesus Wins - The End. He has the Last Say

The world will continue to exalt itself and in turn be drained by its own need for power. But there is *good news*. God is never giving up His position, unmatched and uncontested, despite the world's ambition.

As children of the King, our inheritance, too, has been set. As we walk in obedience to Him, following our beloved Jesus, we cling tightly to the truth of I Corinthians 4:20, "For the Kingdom of God is not just a lot of talk; it is living by God's power."

And in this season and always, we offer a grateful *amen*.

Sat. Dec. 1 ~ 2018

GOD IS ALL-POWERFUL.

Take a moment and write out your own definition for today's attribute of God:

In order to become a doer of the Word, not just a hearer, what can you do today in response to what you have learned about God? (James 1:22)

DOER OF THE WORD

How can you apply what you have learned from the Lord today?

_____
_____
_____
_____

SOCIAL CHALLENGE

// **What is something you can share about today?**

// **Stop and ask God to show you who to share this with today.**

// **Who should you share this with? (Finish sentence below.)**

THIS MESSAGE IS *FOR ALL* BUT IT IS ALSO FOR:

// **Pray over that person(s) or group and ask God for an opportunity and courage to share.**

IF YOU SHARE ON SOCIAL MEDIA
BE SURE TO USE #SACREDHOLIDAYS + TAG @SACREDHOLIDAYS.

SOVEREIGN
by Elizabeth Woodson

PRAISE GOD. REPENT OF SIN. ASK FOR OTHERS + YOURSELF.

YIELD TO GOD TODAY. WAIT + LISTEN.

I love to read, and growing up as a kid, *Choose Your Own Adventure* books were some of my favorites. Honestly, even though the storylines were engaging, they were probably my favorite because I got to choose how the story ended. At a certain point in the story, the book would ask you to make a choice about the direction of the plot. For instance, the book might be about a treasure that's hidden in the next-door neighbor's haunted house. Once the storyline got you into the house, the book would pose the question, "Do you want to check the basement or look upstairs for more clues to where the mysterious golden treasure is hidden?" Now, I wish I could say I would blindly make a decision, but I usually read ahead! Whichever choice ended better is the choice I would make. Like I said, I like knowing how the story is going to end!

Unfortunately, life doesn't offer us opportunities to make decisions based upon future information.

Many times we walk through situations with little to no information on how the situation is going to resolve. It could be health issues, financial issues, or for my beloved singles, just the simple question of whether or not you will get married.

Part of the reason the lack of information is bothersome is because what it really means is that we are not in control. I'll admit, I find comfort in being in control. I enjoy having all the answers because that means I can have the assurance things will go my way every time. But for the past few years, God has been working on my control issues, teaching me to loosen the grip on a life that is ultimately not mine.

I love the stories in Scripture because they reflect the lives of real people with real problems just like mine. In my "control adjustment" season, one story that has encouraged me is the nation of Israel in Exodus 14 and what happens after they leave Egypt. The Israelites had spent 400 years in slavery, and then Moses showed up on the scene. After going back and forth with Pharaoh and orchestrating the manifestation of God's glory through 10 plagues, Moses was able to secure the freedom of the Israelites. Not only were they able to leave free, the Egyptians also showered them with gold, silver, and clothing! They left in style! You would think it was the end of the story, but there was one more piece to their journey the Israelites were completely unaware of.

- **Read Exodus 14:1-4. What did God tell Moses to do and why?**

Turn Back - encamp by the sea - so Pharaoh will pursue them -
Why? God will get glory and show them He is Lord

- **Read Exodus 14:10-12. What was the response of the Israelites?**

   Terrified - cried out
   Questioned Moses

God told Moses to turn the Israelites around and literally back them into a corner! Now, the Israelites didn't know about the conversation God had with Moses. They didn't know <u>God had a plan for what seemed like a death sentence</u>, the impending attack of the Egyptians. The Israelites were afraid, and their candid comments showed it. I wish I could say I respond differently in situations where I feel out of control, but that is not always the case. I don't know about you, but I find comfort in having all the information, and I tend to depend on myself more than I depend on God.

- **How do you feel when you are in a situation where you're not in control of the outcome?**

   Anxious, Angry

I love Moses's response to their fear in verse 13. I would translate this to say, "Don't worry! God's got it. He's about to defeat the Egyptians for good!" What the Israelites failed to remember is that even though they didn't know how the situation was going to work out, God did!

- **Read Exodus 14:15-31 and summarize what happens.**

   Waters part
   Angel holds back enemy w/ fire
   Enemy drowns

- **How do you think the Israelites would have responded to Moses in verses 10-12 if they knew the end of the story?**

   With Praise - Anticipation in a front row seat to see God's splendor & Power.

- **Looking back over your own life, how could you have trusted God better in a season of uncertainty?**

   Prayed
   Worshipped More

Our God is sovereign, which means He controls everything that happens in this world. <u>Nothing takes place that He does not know about, allow to happen, or approve of.</u> With a God who loves us unconditionally, I hope this brings you comfort! In the same way that God ultimately had a plan for the good of the Israelites, His plan for our life is for our good—even when it doesn't feel good. At the end of the day, God's plan for the Israelites was to deliver them from slavery and ultimately to glorify Himself. Ladies, the same is true for the situations in our lives. Whatever we are lacking, God desires to fulfill, but He also desires to bring <u>Himself glory</u> through the miracles He gets to perform. Our moment of weakness requires us to depend on God, giving Him the space to show up and do the impossible in our lives.

- **Describe a time in your life where God has done what seemed to you as impossible.**

    He kept me close to Him while I struggled (struggle) with anxiety. I've seen much progress with anxiety and He's been with me through it all.

The next time you find yourself in a situation where the outcome is unknown, trust God. Trust that He is in control, working out the situation on your behalf, for your good. Whether you need healing, provision, freedom, or simply peace, remember we serve a sovereign God who is able to do beyond what we could ever imagine. All we have to do is trust Him!

Wrap up today by writing down what the following verses teach you about God being sovereign:

- **Proverbs 16:9**

    The Lord establishes our steps though we plan... He overrides

- **Job 42:2**

    God's purpose will be done – Period!

- **Isaiah 55:8-11**

    His ways are different / higher / better

- **Jeremiah 32:27**

    God allows attacks on His people. Angry...

- **Matthew 19:26**

    God does the impossible

GOD IS SOVEREIGN.

Take a moment and write out your own definition for today's attribute of God:

In order to become a doer of the Word, not just a hearer, what can you do today in response to what you have learned about God? (James 1:22)

DOER OF THE WORD

How can you apply what you have learned from the Lord today?

_____
_____
_____
_____

SOCIAL CHALLENGE

// **What is something you can share about today?**

// **Stop and ask God to show you who to share this with today.**

// **Who should you share this with? (Finish sentence below.)**

THIS MESSAGE IS *FOR ALL* BUT IT IS ALSO FOR:

// **Pray over that person(s) or group and ask God for an opportunity and courage to share.**

IF YOU SHARE ON SOCIAL MEDIA
BE SURE TO USE #SACREDHOLIDAYS + TAG @SACREDHOLIDAYS.

JUST
by Leigh Kohler

PRAISE GOD. REPENT OF SIN. ASK FOR OTHERS + YOURSELF.

YIELD TO GOD TODAY. WAIT + LISTEN.

Years ago, I was astonished and saddened to hear the story of a widow from Africa whose relatives, right after her husband's funeral, encroached upon the boundary lines of her property to steal it away. Day after day they threatened her. One day they cornered her children with machetes, scaring them into leaving. She said this was a common problem. People would take advantage of widows' vulnerability and steal their homes and land, leaving them destitute and without the means to provide for their families. Her situation grew increasingly hopeless as she spoke of local authorities looking the other way and doing nothing to bring justice to her situation.

- **Describe a time you've seen or heard about—or experienced firsthand—an injustice being done.**

Joni = Cancer after being paralyzed...

Sometime later, I came across Proverbs 23:10-11, which says, "Don't move an ancient boundary marker, and don't encroach on the fields of the fatherless, for their Redeemer is strong, and He will take up their case against you." Before knowing this woman's story, boundary markers and encroaching on fields didn't have much meaning in my world. Suddenly, this verse had new meaning to me—it took my breath away. Never had I appreciated or loved the justice of God more; it brings me so much joy!

- **Write Proverbs 21:15 in the space below.**

When justice is done, it brings joy to the righteous but terror to evildoers.

One of the most devastating effects of sin is the horrible injustice that takes place under the sun. We look back in history at events like the holocaust, the slave trade, and people being falsely accused of crimes they didn't commit. Yet our hope as Christians comes from our confident assurance in a just God who is going to set all things right.

A.W. Tozer once said, "Justice is not something God has, justice is something God is." God's justice flows from His holy nature. Man's justice can become skewed and perverted because of sin, but God is not capable of any wrongdoing. Proverbs 16:11 says, "Honest scales and balances belong to the Lord; all the weights in the bag are of his making." He's a God who rewards uprightness and punishes sin. It's interesting how the world often scorns the notion of God being a judge. They want to picture him as a cuddly grandpa or nice guy who tolerates sin and looks the other way when we do something wrong. But if God did not punish sin, He would not be good. Deep inside, we want evil to be punished and good to be rewarded. Because we are made in the image of God, we have an innate sense of justice.

- ***Read Isaiah 61:8a. What does the Lord love? What does He hate? Like Father like daughter, notice how you share the same sense of justice.***

> Love → justice
> Hate → Robbery & wrongdoing

I can see this God-given sense of justice in my kids. When they've been hurt or wronged somehow, they run to me. If I look at them, shrug my shoulders, and say, "So what?" they would be outraged. They would question my love and concern for their well-being. Their understanding of my love for them is wrapped-up in the knowledge that I am looking out for them, with a desire to set things right the best I know how. Of course, I don't always get it right—unlike our Heavenly Father!

The ultimate demonstration of God's justice is displayed at the cross. Because God is a righteous and just God, the penalty for our sins had to be paid. There was no way around it. So, God in His mercy, sent His own Son to pay for our sin. He willingly and lovingly humbled Himself, came to this earth and suffered our punishment so that justice could be met. And all of those who put their faith in Jesus for salvation are no longer subject to the punishment of sin and death. Justice was met by our Savior.

- ***Read Isaiah 30:18. There are two things our just God longs to show us. What are they?***

> Graciousness
> Compassion

In our own lives, we will all feel the pain of injustice at some level. We may be taken advantage of or stolen from. We may find ourselves misunderstood, falsely accused, or treated unfairly. Too often, the enemy tempts us to question the character of God, saying a good God would not allow the world to be so complex, so difficult, so deplete of equity and justice. He is always at work, trying to cast a shadow over the goodness of God. Let us not agree with our enemy or call into question God's character. Instead, let's declare like the Psalmist, "The LORD is upright; he is my Rock, and there is no wickedness in Him" (Psalm 92:15).

The widow's story that I spoke of earlier ended wonderfully! She rejoiced as she spoke of God raising up a ministry that came to her aid to fight for justice for her and her children. They put pressure on the police to enforce the law and justice prevailed! The Church has always been God's "Plan A" for redemption in the world, and we must never lose sight of that. Proverbs 31:8 says, "Speak up for those who have no voice, for the justice of all who are dispossessed. Speak up, judge righteously, and defend the cause of the oppressed and needy."

I am so grateful I belong to a God who fights on behalf of all those in need of justice. "Righteousness and justice are the foundation of [His] throne" (Psalm 89:14). Today, let's praise Him and thank Him for being a just God!

GOD IS JUST.

Take a moment and write out your own definition for today's attribute of God:

In order to become a doer of the Word, not just a hearer, what can you do today in response to what you have learned about God? (James 1:22)

DOER OF THE WORD

How can you apply what you have learned from the Lord today?

_____
_____
_____
_____

SOCIAL CHALLENGE

// What is something you can share about today?

// Stop and ask God to show you who to share this with today.

// Who should you share this with? (Finish sentence below.)

THIS MESSAGE IS *FOR ALL* BUT IT IS ALSO FOR:

// Pray over that person(s) or group and ask God for an opportunity and courage to share.

IF YOU SHARE ON SOCIAL MEDIA
BE SURE TO USE #SACREDHOLIDAYS + TAG @SACREDHOLIDAYS.

UNCHANGING (IMMUTABLE)
by Deanna Opheim

PRAISE GOD. REPENT OF SIN. ASK FOR OTHERS + YOURSELF.

YIELD TO GOD TODAY. WAIT + LISTEN.

In my early twenties, when I began to experience some of life's early hardships, my father would attempt to comfort me by saying, "The only thing constant in life is change." I remember chuckling at this notion, maybe even responding with an "Amen!" Although my dad would love to take credit for this quote, the origin has never been confirmed, though it might trace back to the Greek philosopher, Heraclitus of Ephesus. Heraclitus was known for his theories on change; he believed that everything is constantly changing and, the world as we know it, is made up of a bunch of changing things. This theory is actually spot on, right?

- **Does the quote, "The only thing constant in life is change," bring you comfort or make you uneasy? How so?**

  Uneasy - don't like change

Change is a daunting truth for so many; waking up to the unknown is a scary thing. The good news is that the reality of change does not hold its weight against God. One of the most beautiful and comforting attributes of God is that He is immutable; He does not and will not change!

- **Write Malachi 3:6 below.** *I the Lord do not change. So you, the descendants of Jacob, are not destroyed.*

To fully comprehend something that cannot change is impossible for our finite minds, but can we consider this wonder together for a moment, in hopes of knowing our Father better? Let's look at what being immutable instils. Essentially, the immutability of God means it is impossible for His character, His will and His covenant promises, to change. His essence has always been the same and there is no altering His being. He cannot grow or evolve, or even change for the better, because He is already perfect! God cannot improve because He lacks in no area. There never was a time when He was not, and there will never be a time when He will cease to be. Who He was before the beginning of time, is who He is now and forever more (Hebrews 13:8). This is why He says to Moses, "I Am That I Am" (Exodus 3:14).

Everything we know and study about God is meant to push us closer to Him, and ultimately, for us to fall deeper in love with Him. So, when I ponder the immutability of my Father, I am in awe at His never-changing, never-ending love for me. Before the beginning of time, before you were ever a thought on this earth, God's love and promises for you were already established and set in stone!

- ***Jeremiah 1:5 says, "Before I formed you in the womb I knew you . . ." In what way does this verse draw you closer to your Father?***

    He set a place for me at the table knowing I was coming...

Scripture tells us in Isaiah 49:16 that He has written the names of His children on the palms of his hands! God almighty loves you so much, He tattooed your name on His Hand! This shows His never ending, binding convent He has made with His children. When God willed us to be his children, that will does not change!

Charles Spurgeon catalogs his first sermon on the immutability of God. He eloquently puts it: "We cannot tell you what Godhead is. We do not know what substance that is which we call God. It is an existence, it is a being; but what that is, we know not. However, whatever it is, we call it His essence, and that essence never changes." God's character is divinely perfect; it distinguishes Him from every other being as He is perpetually the same. He is subject to no change. This can be hard to comprehend because people are subject to change based on how we act and react towards each other.

- ***Read Numbers 23:19. Unlike God, we change our minds. In what circumstances or surroundings do you find yourself changing? This could be a positive change or negative.***

    Stress, lack of sleep, cycles, no time with the Lord

So often, we strive to win the approval of men by our works, hoping to gain self-worth in return. We make every effort to gain affection, attention, acceptance and love from the people closest to us. Occasionally we mess up and end up losing respect, trust, and even love from our friends and, sometimes, family. Our actions demand a response from the people around us, and those reactions are conditional. Humanly, our love is subject to change towards others depending on what they do to us and what they do for us. But God's love is not capricious; it is not based on conditions. There is NOTHING we can do to lose His love—nothing! His character is unwavering. There is nothing that can separate us from the love of God. His love is unconditional!

- ***James 1:17 says that with God, "there is no variation or shifting shadow." Describe the sense of security this gives you.***

Lastly, let's talk about the promises of God. Have you ever broken a promise? Chances are you have because you are human. Because God is immutable, His covenant promises cannot be broken. We serve a promise keeping God! When God says He will meet all of our needs (Philippians 4:19), we can take that to the bank! We need only to abide and believe in Him. Often we anticipate the outcome of our promises to look a certain way. We don't take into account the means by which the promise is fulfilled. We walk through pain and wonder where the promise is. We forget the promise is in the pain. When we face hardship and crisis, God promises He will see us through! Not even death can interfere with His promises: "to live is Christ and to die is gain" (Philippians 1:21), and "God is faithful to complete the good work He started in you" (Philippians 1:6).

"For the mountains may depart and the hills be removed, but my steadfast love shall not depart from you, and my covenant of peace shall not be removed," says The Lord, who has compassion on you" (Isaiah 54:10).

GOD IS UNCHANGING (IMMUTABLE).

Take a moment and write out your own definition for today's attribute of God:

In order to become a doer of the Word, not just a hearer, what can you do today in response to what you have learned about God? (James 1:22)

DOER OF THE WORD

How can you apply what you have learned from the Lord today?

_____

_____

_____

_____

SOCIAL CHALLENGE

// What is something you can share about today?

// Stop and ask God to show you who to share this with today.

// Who should you share this with? (Finish sentence below.)

THIS MESSAGE IS *FOR ALL* BUT IT IS ALSO FOR:

// Pray over that person(s) or group and ask God for an opportunity and courage to share.

IF YOU SHARE ON SOCIAL MEDIA
BE SURE TO USE #SACREDHOLIDAYS + TAG @SACREDHOLIDAYS.

JEALOUS

PRAISE GOD. REPENT OF SIN. ASK FOR OTHERS + YOURSELF.

YIELD TO GOD TODAY. WAIT + LISTEN.

In college I dated a cute guy named Kyle for six months. I had a nagging sense toward the end of those six months that he wasn't really that into me, and when I eventually voiced my concern, it led to our split during spring finals. I returned home for the summer heartbroken, still wanting so badly for him to care for me as I cared for him.

In August of that summer, I attended a friend's birthday party and saw Kyle again for the first time since we'd broken up. As soon as I noticed he was there, I felt a twinge in my heart that confirmed I wasn't over him yet. He, however, was clearly over me. He spent the entire night following another girl around like a puppy dog, trying to capture her attention. I drove away from the party that night in tears, jealous of the attention he'd given her, wanting so badly to have won his affections for myself.

Even now, years later, I feel a sense of injustice rising up as I type these words, because Kyle and I did eventually get back together, and he eventually became my husband. To recall how his affections turned toward someone else back in the day makes me jealous because, although I know I'm his one-and-only today and in the future, there was a time when I wasn't. I want to have always been his girl!

It's hard not to think of that kind of relational jealousy when I read in Scripture that God is a jealous God. Is God's jealousness like this—the same as ours? I don't think so. Though His jealousy is difficult to wrap our minds around and perhaps one of His greatest and most misunderstood attributes, when we do understand this aspect of Him and how the Messiah is a manifestation of God's jealousy, it is simply breathtaking.

God's jealousy is provoked by one thing. What is that one thing?

- **Read the following and make any key notes you learn about jealousy: Exodus 20:4-6, Exodus 34:12-16, and Deuteronomy 4:23-24.**

- **What is our jealousy typically provoked by?**

- **Is this different from what God's jealousy is provoked by? If so, how is it different?**

Our jealousy is typically provoked by an affront to our sense of justice. When I saw Kyle trying to win the affections of another girl, it stirred feelings of rejection and injustice at not being "chosen." Our jealousy is like this, always exalting self.

God's jealousy is much different. In the passages we read, God's jealousy was provoked when His people gave their affections to idols, when they worshipped and served the created rather than the Creator. His jealousy is borne out of rightful ownership, but it's also borne out of a heart that wants the very best for His children.

He was jealous *for* His people, not jealous of people or even the idols they turned toward. He has never been in competition with anyone or anything. He was jealous for His people's affections because He knew that only He could give them all their hearts longed for. He knew those idols were broken, worthless, and empty and how they would, every single one, eventually break the hearts of those He loved.

His jealousy is also protective. How so?

- **Read Deuteronomy 4:25-28.**

- **What were the consequences of idolatry for the Israelites? In other words, what was God's jealousy attempting to protect them from?**

Notice that Moses speaks prophetically: "You will be scattered." And eventually they were indeed scattered, because they resisted God's jealous protection and His desire to give them what was best.

And yet . . .

God's jealousy is purposeful.

- **What was God's promise to the Israelites through the prophet Ezekiel in Ezekiel 39:21-29?**

He promised their complete restoration. God, in His jealousy for the reconciliation of His people with their God, had a plan. His plan wasn't merely to return the Israelites to their land, although He did indeed do that. His plan wasn't merely to make them a great nation again, although He did indeed do that. His jealousy extended to you and to me. He did not stop until we all had the opportunity to accept the best God could give—Himself.

- **What does God in His jealousy promise in Ezekiel 39:29 and Joel 2:28-32?**

- **Notice the word "afterward" in Joel. After what is the Spirit poured out? Who fulfills this prophetic promise?**

In my jealousy toward the other girl at the party, my heart was turned toward myself with zealous selfishness. God in His jealousy turned towards us with the greatest act of selflessness—sending His Son to us, knowing He would suffer and die at the hands of men. All so we could have the very best and have what most satisfies our souls. All so we could see with our eyes and know deep in our hearts that God's love for us is real and true and farther-reaching than our sin.

It was jealousy that sent Jesus.

GOD IS JEALOUS.

Take a moment and write out your own definition for today's attribute of God:

In order to become a doer of the Word, not just a hearer, what can you do today in response to what you have learned about God? (James 1:22)

DOER OF THE WORD

How can you apply what you have learned from the Lord today?

_____
_____
_____
_____

SOCIAL CHALLENGE

// What is something you can share about today?

// Stop and ask God to show you who to share this with today.

// Who should you share this with? (Finish sentence below.)

THIS MESSAGE IS *FOR ALL* BUT IT IS ALSO FOR:

// Pray over that person(s) or group and ask God for an opportunity and courage to share.

IF YOU SHARE ON SOCIAL MEDIA
BE SURE TO USE #SACREDHOLIDAYS + TAG @SACREDHOLIDAYS.

ETERNAL

by Mary Wiley

PRAISE GOD. REPENT OF SIN. ASK FOR OTHERS + YOURSELF.

YIELD TO GOD TODAY. WAIT + LISTEN.

Forever—what does that even mean today?

In the last few weeks, I've used it to describe the wait in line the grocery store, the drive time to work, how long I plan to live in the house we recently moved into, and the extent of my love for my husband. I use forever synonymously with "a frustratingly long wait" and "until I stop breathing," and you can decide which definition I used for each of the above scenarios.

- **In what context have you used "forever" recently?**

As silly as it is, my idea of forever is often so limited. My little finite brain has a hard time with the idea of anything lasting forever. Yet, Scripture paints the most beautiful picture of eternity. Not only is our God eternally existing, but His eternality is communicated to all His other attributes as well. Our God is eternally faithful to His people and His promises, eternally good, eternally in control, eternally kind, merciful, just, and reigning.

- **Look up the definition of eternal and write it below.**

- **Write Genesis 1:1 below, and notice how God's eternality is the first of His attributes addressed in Scripture.**

- *John also records it in John 1. Jump over to the New Testament and read John's writing in John 1:1-3. What attributes of God are found in these three verses?*

In both of these passages, we don't see, "In the beginning, God was created." Instead, we see that God in His perfection and in His completeness had always been. He was not created, but all the world was created through Him. Here the Greek word for beginning is ἀρχή (archē), and this word is repeated for us in Revelation 22:13. It comes from the root word, "head" or "rule." Isn't it interesting that these passages aren't only telling us that God was present, but that He was always ruling?

- *Look up Revelation 22:13. What does this add to what we read in Genesis 1 and John 1?*

God is the beginning and the end. He is not bound by our ideas of time, and He has always been and will always be. God is eternal, and because He is eternal, we can trust that what He says about the beginning of the world and how it will end is true.

Take your best shot at drawing a timeline of what we've learned so far today:

Read Psalm 90.

Most Bible scholars believe that Moses penned this prayer when God sentenced Israel in the wilderness for their disobedience, complaining, and unbelief (story in Numbers 14). Only Caleb and Joshua would enter the Promised Land alive. In that moment, Moses comforted himself and the people by reminding them of God's eternal nature, the fleeting nature of our lives, the difficulty of accepting the sentence that was placed upon them, and God's faithful love, even when His people disobey.

Read Psalm 90:1-2 again.

The Hebrew term near the end of verse two, translated "everlasting" or "eternity," is found 208 times in Scripture, and it is often used to describe the nature of God's promises to His people. When He sets up covenants, they are for eternity. It also is translated as "permanent" or "perpetual."

What's the big idea in Psalm 90:3-6?

Directly following a reminder of God's eternal nature, we see a reminder of our own mortality. The comparison of our finiteness and God's eternal nature is staggering. Doesn't it make you feel so small? Toward the end of this chapter, we see Moses ask for God to keep their smallness and His eternal faithfulness at the top of His mind.

Even though God's people complained and deserved His wrath, that didn't stop Him from keeping His promise to them. Although only Joshua and Caleb would enter the Promised Land, God kept His promise to deliver them there because He is eternally faithful, and ultimately, God would offer up the ability to live in a land eternally with Him through faith in Jesus and the work He did on the cross. What a reminder we have this season of His eternal nature, His perfect long-standing plan to send Jesus, and the redemption that Jesus brings, allowing us to dwell in a right relationship with our eternal, unchanging God forever.

Take some time to thank God for the eternal, unchanging nature of God - His eternal faithfulness, goodness, and mercy that He has poured out for you.

GOD IS ETERNAL.

Take a moment and write out your own definition for today's attribute of God:

In order to become a doer of the Word, not just a hearer, what can you do today in response to what you have learned about God? (James 1:22)

DOER OF THE WORD

How can you apply what you have learned from the Lord today?

_____
_____
_____
_____

SOCIAL CHALLENGE

// What is something you can share about today?

// Stop and ask God to show you who to share this with today.

// Who should you share this with? (Finish sentence below.)

THIS MESSAGE IS *FOR ALL* BUT IT IS ALSO FOR:

// Pray over that person(s) or group and ask God for an opportunity and courage to share.

IF YOU SHARE ON SOCIAL MEDIA
BE SURE TO USE #SACREDHOLIDAYS + TAG @SACREDHOLIDAYS.

HEALER
by Megan Burns

PRAISE GOD. REPENT OF SIN. ASK FOR OTHERS + YOURSELF.

YIELD TO GOD TODAY. WAIT + LISTEN.

If you have spent any time in a church setting, you are probably very aware that Jesus performed miracles during His time on Earth. He turned water into wine; He multiplied food to feed 5,000; He even healed people. When I think about what it would have been like to see the water turn to wine or the small bit of food feed that many people, I know that I would have been shocked.

I am a lover of logic, and those experiences would not have made sense to my mind, or my eyes for that matter. Even though such miracles were amazing and awe-worthy, I am confident they didn't even begin to compare to when Jesus healed people.

It is my belief that every single person needs to be healed of something—maybe it's physical, maybe it's mental, maybe it's a deep wound, maybe it's a way of thinking. Each one of us has something we need healing from or some place in our heart that needs more freedom.

I think many of us are aware of this fact. We have this sense deep down in our souls that there is a better way. We believe in a life of more joy, more freedom, more health, more confidence, more peace, and we desire that for ourselves.

In my experience, even people who aren't consciously aware of the fact that they need healing oftentime verbalize what they need healing from. We complain, we judge, we self help, we go into denial, we process it unceasingly with friends. And if I can be completely honest, most of the time we get it wrong by turning to prayer and our faith in God last.

- **What do you need to be healed from?**

Anxiety, Depression, Negativity, Judgementalism, Pride, Selfishness, Complaints

Here is the deal, friend. If we aren't seeking the face of the Lord first and praying desperate prayers for healing, then we are missing the mark. The fact of the matter is, even though we can get amazing advice from friends, we can read incredibly insightful and soul-filling books, we can work on ourselves until the end of time, the only person who can ultimately heal us is Jesus. → *Can He not heal through doctors or meds or self-awareness?*

One of my favorite stories about healing is in Mark 5. It's the story of the woman who had been sick for twelve years. Twelve years, friend.

- **Take a moment and read her story in Mark 5:24-34 and note parts of the story that stand out to you:**

- **Let's do some math to let that sink in. How many months are twelve years? How many weeks? How many days?**

It says she had basically spent all of her money going to doctor after doctor, but instead of getting better she continued to get worse.

- **Can you relate to this woman in any way? Reflect on your own story below.**

Have you gotten test after test done, only to receive no answer? Have you tried prescriptions, natural remedies, therapies, and all the things you can possibly do, all with no success? Do you often feel hopeless, like it may never get better? Do you wonder if this is just what the rest of your life will look like? Or maybe yours isn't a physical sickness, but something else that persists no matter how hard you try. You are not alone, friend, and I am so very sorry that you are going through this.

The thing that stands out to me the most about this woman is that she has so much hope. In verse 28 she is convinced: "If I just touch His clothes, I will be healed."

Part of the reason this is so shocking is, culturally speaking, if she were to touch His clothes, He would be considered unclean just like she was.

She did it anyway.

Gosh, that part is so convicting every single time I read it. For one, she didn't lose hope. She knew in every part of her being that Jesus <u>could</u> heal her.

- **Do you believe that for your situation?**

Could yes
Will~?

In transparency, I believe Jesus heals, but I don't live every minute of every day like I'm convinced of this truth. Because if I did truly believe that He could heal me, then I wouldn't feel so hopeless all the dang time. Right? Does this resonate with you too?

When she knew she had been healed, she wasn't the only one who noticed. It says that Jesus could tell something had happened, so He stopped in His tracks and asked who had touched Him. I would've been so nervous! She risked her pride and her safety when she fell at His feet and confessed it was her.

- **What did Jesus say to her in Mark 5:34?**

Whenever I read this verse, I take a big, deep exhale every single time. Be freed from your suffering because your faith has healed you. Isn't that the ache of our soul?

Maybe the person who is suffering physically isn't you but rather someone you love. It can feel so powerless and scary sometimes knowing there is literally nothing you can do but pray. Those moments are so holy, friend. Please don't miss them. When we realize how much we need God, it puts everything in its rightful place. We recognize our weakness, and we depend on His strength.

Are you able to have hope again? Are you able to believe that He can heal you or your loved one? Are you so convinced He can do it, that you would be bold enough to set your pride and ego aside and pray radically to Him?

- **What has the Lord shown you in this story of the woman who needed healing? Is there something He is asking of you? Is there something He is trying to tell you?**

Regardless of where you are on your journey to freedom from your suffering, please know that you aren't alone. I personally know how lonely it can feel at times, but it is so vital to remember that even when we are lonely, we really aren't alone. He is for you and your good and has more freedom for you than you can even imagine. Sometimes the end of the story doesn't look like how we would've written it ourselves. It's so painful, heartbreaking, and makes you question a million different things. Even in those moments there is something in our souls that knows He is for us. That is faith, friend. It is our faith that heals us.

- **Read and write out Psalm 30:2.**

My prayer for you is that you can have faith even when it doesn't make sense. I am praying for you so very much and believe for complete and total healing for you and your loved ones. I can't wait for the moment when He says to you, "Daughter, your faith has healed you. Go in peace and be freed!"

GOD IS HEALER.

Take a moment and write out your own definition for today's attribute of God:

In order to become a doer of the Word, not just a hearer, what can you do today in response to what you have learned about God? (James 1:22)

DOER OF THE WORD

How can you apply what you have learned from the Lord today?

_____
_____
_____
_____

SOCIAL CHALLENGE

// What is something you can share about today?

// Stop and ask God to show you who to share this with today.

// Who should you share this with? (Finish sentence below.)

THIS MESSAGE IS *FOR ALL* BUT IT IS ALSO FOR:

// Pray over that person(s) or group and ask God for an opportunity and courage to share.

IF YOU SHARE ON SOCIAL MEDIA
BE SURE TO USE #SACREDHOLIDAYS + TAG @SACREDHOLIDAYS.

FAITHFUL
by Jamie Ivey

PRAISE GOD. REPENT OF SIN. ASK FOR OTHERS + YOURSELF.

YIELD TO GOD TODAY. WAIT + LISTEN.

In our second year of marriage, my husband Aaron and I moved from Houston to Nashville. We took the first of many leaps of faith in our marriage and were confident we were doing precisely what God had in store for us in that season of our lives. We both left full-time jobs to pursue ministry in a way that seemed out-of-the-box and maybe a tad bit unwise for a young, married couple. The seemingly wild part was our lack of answers to questions like, "But you don't have full-time jobs lined up where you are moving?" and, "How will you pay your bills the first month?"

We planned for the unknown, we prepared for the next few years, and we developed a rock-solid plan of what life would look like for us over the next five years. I would work full-time in teaching, and Aaron would pursue his band full-time. Seems rock-solid, right?

The most significant part of the plan we had developed was our timeframe for having children. Together we decided we needed five more years under our belt in life and marriage before embarking on the new adventure of being a mommy and daddy. This decision would put us at that seven-year mark for our marriage, a time we would both be established in careers and probably be much more suitable for the role of parent.

Two months into our five-year plan, it fell apart because I found myself pregnant. (Now I understand the saying, "You'll never be fully ready for parenting!") This new life in my belly should be remarkable, right?! We're a happily married couple, and God has gifted us with this child. Except our plans didn't include a child. Our plans included working, ministry, and waiting five years for parenting.

Unexpectedly becoming pregnant was one of the greatest gifts God has ever given us. Besides the 9 lb. 11 oz. (yes, you read that right) bundle of joy that made us a family of three, that season developed something in our family that has become a building block for so many other seasons in our marriage.

God used this unexpected situation in our lives to take us to places where we had to trust Him daily for our needs.

- **Have you ever found yourself in a place of needing to trust Him daily for your needs? Share more below.**

God was always faithful. However, just because God was faithful doesn't mean life was always comfortable.

I left my teaching job, Aaron continued to pursue his music, and God remained faithful. We were so poor I needed government assistance to have our cute 9 lb. 11 oz. (I still feel the need to remind people of this number!) bundle of joy, and the only way our rent got paid that December was because my husband sold one of his guitars. He plays music for a living, so guitars are somewhat important—but so was a roof over our heads and food in our mouths. I still get teary-eyed when I think of the grown-up decisions we had to make during those months of hardly any money coming in!

But what happened in our lives during those nine months was that we saw how God loves and cares about us—in spite of our plans not lining up with His plans. We were forced to rely strictly on Him to keep us afloat. We prayed more than ever for Him to be our source of joy, comfort, and security.

In that season of struggle, we learned God is trustworthy. He didn't abandon us then, and He won't abandon us in the future.

Friends, God is faithful to you even when you feel as though this isn't the direction you thought your life would go.

Friends, God is faithful to you even when the outcome is different from how you imagined.

Friends, God is faithful to you because it's in His character to be faithful. He has no other option and no other way of treating His daughters.

I often wonder if the disciples doubted God's faithfulness to them as they watched their best friend die on a cross. Did they begin to question everything that Jesus had taught them over the past three years? Were there murmurs of doubt and confusion among the disciples? Did they feel as though God had left them in their highest time of need?

- **Read and write out 1 Corinthians 1:9.**

The beautiful thing about God is that His faithfulness to us doesn't hinge on what we think His faithfulness should look like to us. God can do nothing but be faithful to His children. So when you feel as though God has fallen through and hasn't kept His end of the deal, you forget that faithfulness is a character trait of His that He can't not possess.

As Jesus was dying on the cross, the disciples might have wondered if God had left them, and yet we know that God was so faithful to them during those moments. He was fulfilling a promise to His people at that moment. He was devoted to all of us at that moment.

Whatever struggle you might be in right now, know that we serve a God who can do nothing but be faithful. The outcome might not be what you wanted, the journey might be bumpy and miserable, the hurts might be intense, but friend, know that God has not left you, He is for you, and He is faithful.

- ***Share about a time God was faithful in a way you didn't understand at the time but appreciate now.***

Thirteen years later, we are still standing on the faithfulness of God. Even though that year was full of challenges and unknowns, God proved Himself to be faithful to us, and we continue to build our house on the solid rock—the Rock that will never fail us.

GOD IS FAITHFUL.

Take a moment and write out your own definition for today's attribute of God:

In order to become a doer of the Word, not just a hearer, what can you do today in response to what you have learned about God? (James 1:22)

DOER OF THE WORD

How can you apply what you have learned from the Lord today?

_____
_____
_____
_____

SOCIAL CHALLENGE

// **What is something you can share about today?**

// **Stop and ask God to show you who to share this with today.**

// **Who should you share this with? (Finish sentence below.)**

THIS MESSAGE IS *FOR ALL* BUT IT IS ALSO FOR:

// **Pray over that person(s) or group and ask God for an opportunity and courage to share.**

IF YOU SHARE ON SOCIAL MEDIA
BE SURE TO USE #SACREDHOLIDAYS + TAG @SACREDHOLIDAYS.

SURPASSING ORDINARY (TRANSCENDENT)
by Andi Andrew

PRAISE GOD. REPENT OF SIN. ASK FOR OTHERS + YOURSELF.

YIELD TO GOD TODAY. WAIT + LISTEN.

Millions of eyes were glued to their televisions across the world to watch the wedding of Prince Harry and Megan Markle as they became the Duke and Duchess of Sussex. I was in Melbourne, Australia, all alone in my hotel room, glued to the picture of pomp and pageantry that was unfolding on the world's stage. This wedding was like none other that I'd ever seen. Bishop Michael Curry preached the unadulterated Gospel, and every little detail throughout exuded hope, reconciliation and, most of all, love.

This wedding came at a time that the world desperately needed a little bit of hope to move into our neighborhoods. Just a day earlier at Santa Fe High School in Texas, yet another mass school shooting took place, breaking our hearts while throwing more chaos into the already brewing caldron of hot mess. Racism, sexism, wars, rumors of wars, political debates, and division; the list literally feels endless. The times we are living in can be jarring, often confronting and painful to behold. It's no wonder people were glued to their televisions to watch the redemptive story of an ordinary, American, biracial girl, receive a crown as she married into royalty. We needed this story.

- **Read Ecclesiastes 3:10. What beautiful thing has God planted in your heart?**

There is something in the human heart that longs for the Kingdom of God to come now in tangible ways into our lives. It's our homing beacon that is looking for what is real—the eternal. Our hearts are searching for what will last forever. We long for the fairy tale of redemption to be true—and it is true. A transcendent, unreachable, unknowable God who is far beyond our human understanding, stooped low to love us, redeem us, to save us, to touch us, to walk with us. He has placed a crown upon our heads, satisfied our desires with good things, and is continually renewing our lives, even in the midst of pain and turmoil.

Romans 11:33-36 says, "Oh, the depth of the riches of the wisdom and knowledge of God. How unsearchable his judgments, and his paths beyond tracing out! Who has known the mind of the Lord? Or who has been his counselor? Who has ever given to God, that God should repay him? For from him and through him and to him are all things. To him is the glory forever!"

- **The tale end of the above Scripture says, "To Him is the glory forever!" What can you do today to bring glory to our almighty, transrendent God?**

I saw Jesus in a new way the day I saw The Passion of The Christ. This wasn't just a movie; I found myself wondering how and why the God of the universe would transcend space and time to rescue me? Why would the very Word, the Living Expression who was with God at the very beginning of creation, why would He leave His heavenly throne to give His life for me . . . for you . . . for us? The Message puts it this way, "The Word became flesh and blood, and moved into the neighborhood. We saw the glory with our own eyes, the one-of-a-kind glory, like Father, like Son, Generous inside and out, true from start to finish" (John 1:14).

He became a fragile baby—God, wrapped in flesh. He lowered Himself to walk a mile in our shoes. Yet, at the same time He is transcendent. He goes beyond our limits of human experience and knowledge, beyond earthly categories and understanding, independent of the world and our way of doing things. He is Holy and untouchable, yet, He became like us so that we could reach out and touch Him. God is our incomprehensible Creator Who moves beyond time and space, surpassing and exceeding our ordinary human limits. He is righteous and just. He is vastly unsearchable, unknowable, and unfathomable . . . yet He stooped low and seeks to be known by us. This heavenly paradox is too good to be true!

- **Though it's difficult to wrap our hearts and minds around the awesomeness of God (after all, He really is beyond amazing!), jot down a few words that describe who He is to you.**

A transcendent God is too holy for our sin, and therefore must turn His face away from us, yet He chose to send His Son, turning His face toward us. He desires to walk in the cool of the garden with us, close to us, connected to the very ones He has created to be with in relationship. This is the very reason His Son Jesus came to rescue us, washing us clean by His blood, and bringing us home as Sons and Daughters—He is our righteousness. This is all too wonderful to behold—too overwhelming to fathom with our finite minds, yet our transcendent Holy God has broken through the barriers of our sin, drawing us close to His heart.

Recently, one of my sons asked me, "If God has always existed, who created Him? " To which I said, "Um, uh, well . . . I guess that's one of the questions we'll have to ask God when we get to heaven." Good answer right? It's a question that still boggles my mind to this day. I can't wrap my finite mind around the reality that He has always existed. That He speaks and galaxies appear. And on top of all that, He wants to be with me, all of me.

Our transcendent God has made Himself known to us. In the midst of this season, sit and ponder how the God of the universe stooped low, the Word made flesh and blood—vulnerable and tangible, moving into the neighborhood to walk with you, love you and rescue you. The story of His "kingdom come" is real.

GOD IS TRANSCENDENT.

Take a moment and write out your own definition for today's attribute of God:

In order to become a doer of the Word, not just a hearer, what can you do today in response to what you have learned about God? (James 1:22)

DOER OF THE WORD

How can you apply what you have learned from the Lord today?

....
....
....
....

SOCIAL CHALLENGE

// What is something you can share about today?

// Stop and ask God to show you who to share this with today.

// Who should you share this with? (Finish sentence below.)

THIS MESSAGE IS *FOR ALL* BUT IT IS ALSO FOR:

// Pray over that person(s) or group and ask God for an opportunity and courage to share.

IF YOU SHARE ON SOCIAL MEDIA
BE SURE TO USE #SACREDHOLIDAYS + TAG @SACREDHOLIDAYS.

TRUTHFUL
by Katie Orr

PRAISE GOD. REPENT OF SIN. ASK FOR OTHERS + YOURSELF.

YIELD TO GOD TODAY. WAIT + LISTEN.

My husband and I have moved a lot since we've been married. This also means that we've been house shopping several times. During our very first house-shopping experience, I felt like we were walking in blind. Thankfully, we had parents who helped out in the process by giving advice and helping us examine the homes we were interested in.

Though I do not consider myself a house-buying-pro, a theme I've picked up on throughout the years of house shopping is to stay away from homes with any sort of foundation issue. It may be a beautiful house, situated perfectly on a quiet cul-de-sac, but if something is wrong with the foundation, it calls into question the quality of the rest of the house, regardless of how it looks. And even if the rest of the house is built well, a crack in the foundation will eventually take the rest of the house down with it.

The importance of the foundation doesn't only apply to the housing market, our spiritual life is also dependent on and affected by the foundation of what we believe about God. As A.W. Tozer so rightly stated in his book, *The Knowledge of the Holy*, "What comes into our minds when we think about God is the most important thing about us."

- **What is the first thing that comes to your mind when you think about God?**

Our view of God is the foundation of our lives, and unfortunately so many of us are on shaky ground. Our foundation is incomplete and poured out all wrong. Though God is the ultimate and only true Truth, we wonder if He truly is who He claims to be. Part of this is because we have a tendency to try to understand God through who we know already: our parents, our friends, our pastor, our leaders. Yet all of mankind—which includes the ones we look up to the most—is unwittingly inconsistent at best and cunningly deceitful at worst. From a simple omission of details to the intricate, intentional deceptions, not one of us is completely and constantly truthful—especially compared to the absolute truthfulness and trustworthiness of our God.

- **Read Jeremiah 17:5-9. What is God's antidote to trusting in humans (verses 7-8)?**

So, in order to move toward a more sure foundation, we each must fight the tendency to allow our experience of human interaction to taint the reality of who God is, and replace these thoughts with the objective truths of God we find in the Bible. Though the best person I know is still tempted to skirt truth if it makes life easier, my God never lies (Titus 1:2). Though some may tell me one thing today, only to change their tune tomorrow, the truth of the LORD is everlasting (Psalm 117:2). And though many go back on their promises, leaving me uncertain if I can trust them again, my God is a steadfast, covenant-keeper who encourages me to take hold of all He has promised (Hebrews 6:18).

God is the absolute essence of what is true. It is out of character for Him to do anything false, or even to cast a shadow of deceit. And this is crucially important for us to hold on to. If we are honest with ourselves, we can see that much of our disobedience and lack of wholehearted devotion to God stems back to our doubt that God is truth. Because if God is not truth, then He cannot be trusted. If we allow doubt of God's truthfulness to creep in and set root into our hearts, that doubt will erode at the foundation of every other characteristic of who He is.

- **Have you ever stumbled because you doubted the truth of God? How did He draw you back to Himself?**

I've found the more I focus on building my foundation of who God is, through regular time in His Word, deep connections with His people, and doing the work of conforming my beliefs to the truth of God's Word, the easier it is to say yes to His good commands. The more accurate my view of God is, the greater my affection for Him and the easier it is to follow His good plan for my life, as spelled out in His Word. As my foundational beliefs of God grow to become more and more sure and true and right in my mind, the less and less the trials and temptations of this world affect me. In fact, when I hold fiercely to my Lord's veracity—the truthfulness of who He is—the difficulties I encounter drive me closer to Him.

- **Write down Psalm 111:7-8.**

GOD IS TRUTHFUL.

Take a moment and write out your own definition for today's attribute of God:

In order to become a doer of the Word, not just a hearer, what can you do today in response to what you have learned about God? (James 1:22)

DOER OF THE WORD

How can you apply what you have learned from the Lord today?

....
....
....
....

SOCIAL CHALLENGE

// What is something you can share about today?

// Stop and ask God to show you who to share this with today.

// Who should you share this with? (Finish sentence below.)

THIS MESSAGE IS *FOR ALL* BUT IT IS ALSO FOR:

// Pray over that person(s) or group and ask God for an opportunity and courage to share.

IF YOU SHARE ON SOCIAL MEDIA
BE SURE TO USE #SACREDHOLIDAYS + TAG @SACREDHOLIDAYS.

COMFORTER
by Sarah Mae

PRAISE GOD. REPENT OF SIN. ASK FOR OTHERS + YOURSELF.

YIELD TO GOD TODAY. WAIT + LISTEN.

I had to make the decision to stop medical treatment for mom. She was in the hospital for complications with her heart and her liver, and everything was just falling apart. She had stage 3 cirrhosis of the liver due to twenty ears of alcohol abuse. She had been sober around nine years when she ended up in the hospital. She was unable to communicate her needs. The doctors kept telling me to start considering "comfort measures." It was agonizing.

I finally made the decision to have her taken to a hospice where she was to die in "comfort." Once she was there, there didn't seem to be any comfort. She was yelling on and off, moaning and the hospice staff couldn't get a hold of the doctor to get her pain relief. It felt like a nightmare.

After a few hours they finally gave her something, but throughout the night she would yell or moan and I kept crying and praying and feeling like I was killing her. *Agonizing.* The next morning, she was still alive, but quiet. More meds. No more moaning. The doctor came in to see her and I asked him how long it would take for her body to die, and he said that without food or water it could take up to 5-7 days. What? 5-7 days! She was just going to starve to death, and I was going to let this happen? Plus I had to leave the next day to get home to my family who was in Pennsylvania (my mom was in Florida). She would die alone.

Agonizing.

I got a call from my in-laws who also lived in Pennsylvania but were providentially in Florida at the same time I was. Their trip to Florida, only four hours from where I was, had been planned for months in advance. They asked if they could come and be with me while I was with my mom. *Yes.* They came to the hospice and my father-in-law offered to stay with my mom so my mother-in-law and I could go to my mom's apartment. I honestly don't remember why I wanted to go there, but I did and so we went. I walked through the apartment and crawled onto my mom's bed and just cried. We went back to the hospice and a counselor came to the room and asked if I had any questions. I told her I didn't. My MIL said to the counselor, "The doctor said it would take 5-7 days for her to die, is that true?" And the counselor said, "No. Do you hear the sound in her lungs? That's her lungs shutting down. She could die today."

Hope.

That counselor gave us hope that I could be with my mom as she left this world. My in-laws hugged me goodbye so I could be alone with my mom, and they left.

Just a few hours later I could tell she was going to go soon. I pulled a chair up to her bed and I held her hand, played her music, rubbed her head, and told her it was okay. Her eyes stopped moving.

Her breath got slower.

And like a clock winding down, her breaths slowed and then, stopped.

She went into the arms of Jesus.

And I got to be there to see her go.

I tell you this story because even though it was agonizing, God was present in all of it. And He wasn't just present, He was my comforter in the pain.

- **Read 2 Corinthians 1:3-4 and note what you learn about comfort below.**

One of the many reasons God comforts us is so that we can comfort others.

- ***Who in your life could use some comfort today? How could you comfort them?***

The Bible tells us that God is the Father of mercies and all comfort, who comforts us in *all* our affliction. He does this so we will, in turn, be able to comfort those who are in *any* affliction with the comfort we received from Him.

God showed up as Comforter to me through my in-laws, through the hospice counselor, and through His peace which surpasses all understanding. It was not a coincidence that my in-laws planned a trip to Florida, only four hours from where I was, months before my mom was in the hospital. It wasn't a coincidence that my MIL asked the counselor if it was true that it would take several days for mom's body to shut down, and for that counselor to have the insight and knowledge to tell us she could die that day. And it was God in His kindness and mercy that I was able to be with my mom as she died, so she wouldn't have to die alone. None of this was chance. All of it was orchestrated by a God who loves us and wants to comfort us in our affliction.

I know some of you are reading this and you're thinking, "Well, things don't always work out like this." You're right. One of the prayers I prayed and begged God to answer was that my mom would know I was there and that she would acknowledge my presence. And yet, I was there, and through all the agonizing decision-making and pain and exhaustion, God was with me, and He was with her, and He brought comfort to us both.

The thing is, I could have missed His comfort if I stayed stuck on the fact that she didn't acknowledge me. I have learned this instead:

Open your eyes, even in the pain, and see that He is with you.

Open your eyes, even in the exhaustion, and see that He is holding you.

Open your eyes, even in the impossible decisions you have to make, and see that He is there, in you, the Holy Spirit, our Comforter.

We are never alone or on our own. And as we receive His comfort and as we learn more and more to trust the Comforter in us, we will be able to comfort others in their pain. He will comfort through us. What a gift!

- **Read John 14:16 in the King James version. How long does Jesus say His gift—His Comforter—will abide with us?**

Whatever hard thing you're going through, whatever difficult decision or agonizing situation you're facing, remember, we serve a God who is the Father of mercy and comfort, who delights to comfort His children, and who delights when we comfort one another.

You are never alone, and you never suffer alone.

GOD IS OUR COMFORTER.

Take a moment and write out your own definition for today's attribute of God:

In order to become a doer of the Word, not just a hearer, what can you do today in response to what you have learned about God? (James 1:22)

DOER OF THE WORD

How can you apply what you have learned from the Lord today?

_____
_____
_____
_____

SOCIAL CHALLENGE

// What is something you can share about today?

// Stop and ask God to show you who to share this with today.

// Who should you share this with? (Finish sentence below.)

THIS MESSAGE IS *FOR ALL* BUT IT IS ALSO FOR:

// Pray over that person(s) or group and ask God for an opportunity and courage to share.

IF YOU SHARE ON SOCIAL MEDIA
BE SURE TO USE #SACREDHOLIDAYS + TAG @SACREDHOLIDAYS.

GOOD

by Ashley Jackson

PRAISE GOD. REPENT OF SIN. ASK FOR OTHERS + YOURSELF.

YIELD TO GOD TODAY. WAIT + LISTEN.

I grabbed my knee in sheer panic. I knew it had gone out of socket again; trying to move it was excruciating. The day before, while attempting a lunge, I slipped on a baby blanket and fell, and my knee cap moved to the side of my leg! As the firemen and paramedics carefully carried me down the 52 steps of our third story apartment, I tried my best not to scream with every jostle. Here I was again, knowing exactly what I was in for.

My husband rushed in wide-eyed—*oh no not again!*—and we cried out to God like never before: "Just put the knee back on Lord; just give us a miracle, please Lord, please." But the miracle never came and we had to go through the entire process once more—the ambulance, the hospital, and anesthesia to reset my knee.

- **Read Psalm 27:13-14. Describe a time your patience was tested while waiting for something good to happen.**

As my dad sat in the living room with my kids, he was filled with compassion as he watched me get wheeled out. I had the thought that if my earthly father had the power to put my knee back on, he would have. Why wouldn't my heavenly Father do this for me?

As I returned home again, I wrestled with my thoughts toward God and His goodness, for this seemed to be the icing on the cake to what has been nothing but a season of trials. Suddenly a quiet peace came over me. Reflecting on all the good things God has done for me and who He's been to me year after year, I knew I was faced with a choice. I could do it with Him or without Him. I could believe He was still good or allow myself to become embittered and cold, pushing Him away. The choice was easy; no matter what, I'd rather walk this hard road with Him.

- **Philippians 4:8 says, "Finally, brothers and sisters, whatever is true, whatever is noble, whatever is right, whatever is pure, whatever is lovely, whatever is admirable—if anything is excellent or praiseworthy—think about such things." Write down three "excellent and praiseworthy" things God has done for you in the past.**

When we use the word "good" in our daily lives, we say things like, "I had a good day," which means our day was carefree, fun, or easy. When we say someone is a "good friend," we refer to how they really "get" us and how close we feel to them. We use phrases like "good as new" or "good job." We even call people "good Samaritans." But what does it really mean for God to be good?

If we believe that goodness is always tied to a feeling of pleasure or ease, what happens when life doesn't feel that way? Or what do we do when God doesn't intervene, when we know He could? Although God does many *good* things on our behalf (Psalm 31:19), is the source of all *good* gifts (James 1:17), has *good* works prepared in advance for us (Eph. 2:10), and works everything for the *good of* those who love Him (Romans 8:28), it is not what He does or does not do that makes Him good, it is who He is by nature. Even when life feels anything but good, we can run to Him and trust Him in spite of our circumstances.

- ***Write down Psalm 34:8.***

You can't taste and see what's really going on from a long distance away. You must get close. It is an invitation to intimacy, to take part in knowing God personally. A taste, in essence, is a test to see what something is like. It's been said that faith is the soul's taste. His peace, His faithfulness, His joy, His goodness—even when everything in life seems to be crashing around us—is all we need for everlasting joy. We can't be told about it; we have to experience it for ourselves.

We all come to a crossroads in life where we're faced with the question, "If God is good, why does this feel so bad?" It's in those moments we need to run to Him and not from Him, to spend time knowing Him, tasting and seeing His goodness for ourselves—not only hearing about it from secondhand sources. When you have known for yourself the goodness of God, you're devoted for life. Even when circumstances or the enemy tries to throw every last thing at you to get you to mistrust God's goodness, a rising determination of faith in your heart will say, "I remain confident of this: I WILL see the goodness of the Lord in the land of the living" (Psalm 27:13).

GOD IS GOOD.

Take a moment and write out your own definition for today's attribute of God:

In order to become a doer of the Word, not just a hearer, what can you do today in response to what you have learned about God? (James 1:22)

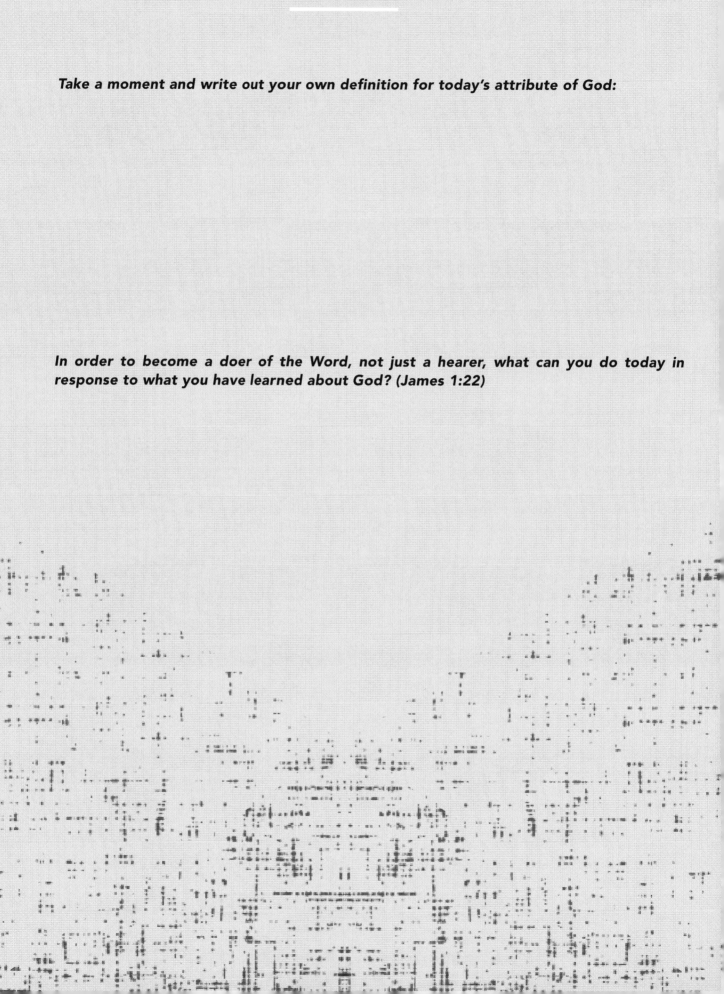

DOER OF THE WORD

How can you apply what you have learned from the Lord today?

_____
_____
_____
_____

SOCIAL CHALLENGE

// **What is something you can share about today?**

// **Stop and ask God to show you who to share this with today.**

// **Who should you share this with? (Finish sentence below.)**

THIS MESSAGE IS *FOR ALL* BUT IT IS ALSO FOR:

// **Pray over that person(s) or group and ask God for an opportunity and courage to share.**

IF YOU SHARE ON SOCIAL MEDIA
BE SURE TO USE #SACREDHOLIDAYS + TAG @SACREDHOLIDAYS.

RIGHTEOUS
by Remi Onayemi

PRAISE GOD. REPENT OF SIN. ASK FOR OTHERS + YOURSELF.

YIELD TO GOD TODAY. WAIT + LISTEN.

- **According to Revelation 16:7, God's actions are always right and just. Do you believe this? Why or why not?**

If I'm honest, within my Christian walk, I have struggled to believe this truth. In a world that is often filled with heartache, suffering, oppression, and injustice—even among those who name the name of Christ—it has been difficult to wrap my mind around the fact that our righteous God's actions are always loving, right, and just. In fact, I've frequently found myself crying out, "Lord, I believe; help my unbelief" (Mark 9:24)!

How can a righteous and sovereign God allow His image bearers to endure unhappiness, persecution, physical harm, psychological trauma, grief, or inequity for lengthy periods of time? Have you ever found yourself wondering similar things? If so, you are not alone.

- **Read Psalm 10:1 and Habakkuk 1:2-3. Are you encouraged to know you're not alone in your lack of understand or feelings of lament?**

The start of the human civilization began in a garden paradise of pure perfection. The righteous One of heaven fashioned the first female and male. Together, they were meant to enjoy the unblemished harmony of a right relationship with God, with His creation, and with one another. Joy comes when we remember our world was not created to be this way.

In this beautifully vast garden, the image bearers of God were only given one rule: "The Lord God took the man and put him in the Garden of Eden to work it and keep it. And the Lord God commanded the man, saying, 'You may surely eat of every tree of the garden, but of the tree of the knowledge of good and evil you shall not eat, for in the day that you eat of it you shall surely die'" (Genesis 2:15-17).

- ***What was the one rule God gave to mankind?***

In Genesis 3, mankind was deceived by the lies and craftiness of the devil. They believed God withheld good from them, therefore, they willingly rebelled against the perfect, loving, and righteous King, and ate of the forbidden tree.

Though Satan intended evil, God intended good. The Lord's predetermined plan was to use this situation for His great glory and the good of all who would trust in Him for help.

- ***Read 2 Timothy 1:9. When did God create a plan to redeem the world through Christ Jesus?***

Thanks be to God! Long before Adam and Eve rebelled—before the creation of the world—the One who always does what is right and just had a plan (through Christ's life, death, burial, resurrection, and ascension) to redeem mankind back to Himself.

- ***Read Psalm 89:14 and write it below.***

The truth is God does see, He is concerned, and He is at work, because He is the righteous Judge of all the earth. When our hearts cry out—"How long, O Lord?"—it is because we are homesick and longing to return to the perfect paradise and presence that mankind lost in Genesis 3. In fact, one might say that every effort toward human progress has simply been an effort to regain what we lost in our exile from Eden.

The enemy intends suffering for evil, but the righteous One intends it for good. Often, we are tempted to define "good" in terms of comfort, health, and happiness, yet God defines it as being conformed to the image of Christ.

Thankfully, Christians have a God who understands our suffering because He Himself has suffered. Enduring suffering is part of Christlikeness. We have a God who genuinely loves and cares about us. Our sufferings affect His heart in the same way that a child's suffering would concern her loving parents.

In Psalm 56:8 David writes, *"You keep track of all my sorrows. You have collected all my tears in your bottle. You have recorded each one in your book."*

Additional questions may persist in the face of extreme evil, oppression, and injustice. For example, why doesn't the righteous Judge bring about swift justice for the wicked?

The truth is, our righteous God's delayed justice allows mankind time to repent.

2 Peter 3:8b-9 reads, "A day is like a thousand years to the Lord, and a thousand years is like a day. The Lord isn't really being slow about his promise, as some people think. No, he is being patient for your sake. He does not want anyone to be destroyed, but wants everyone to repent."

All throughout human history we see stories of God granting grace to some who truly deserved swift justice.

Consider Saul, a man known for murder and the torment of Christians. God transformed him, changed his name to Paul, and used him to preach the Gospel message of love, forgiveness, and hope to the nations.

Similarly, John Newton was a British sailor who promoted and profited from the wicked and murderous transatlantic slave trade. Later, God transformed him into a man who repented of his sin and renounced his loathsome profit. Newtown lived on to compose the beautiful and well-known hymn, "Amazing Grace."

We would do well to reflect upon our own stories of grace and remember the ways God showed patience with us rather than swift justice.

Write a prayer thanking God for specific times in your life where He showed you grace and mercy instead of His swift justice.

Read the following verses—Psalm 145:17; Jeremiah 9:23-24; 2 Corinthians 4:8-9; Isaiah 25:8. What do these verses teach you about...

- **The Righteousness Of God:**

- **Yourself:**

When God's justice does not come swiftly, He is putting His grace, mercy, and patience on display. We must remember that the suffering we experience in this world is only temporary. Yet, the righteous King's final judgment upon evil for those who refuse to repent—and His final relief of the Christian's suffering—will last forever.

"I will give to the Lord the thanks due to his righteousness, and I will sing praise to the name of the Lord, the Most High." Psalm 7:17

GOD IS RIGHTEOUS.

Take a moment and write out your own definition for today's attribute of God:

In order to become a doer of the Word, not just a hearer, what can you do today in response to what you have learned about God? (James 1:22)

DOER OF THE WORD

How can you apply what you have learned from the Lord today?

_____
_____
_____
_____

SOCIAL CHALLENGE

// **What is something you can share about today?**

// **Stop and ask God to show you who to share this with today.**

// **Who should you share this with? (Finish sentence below.)**

THIS MESSAGE IS *FOR ALL* BUT IT IS ALSO FOR:

// **Pray over that person(s) or group and ask God for an opportunity and courage to share.**

IF YOU SHARE ON SOCIAL MEDIA
BE SURE TO USE #SACREDHOLIDAYS + TAG @SACREDHOLIDAYS.

HOLY

PRAISE GOD. REPENT OF SIN. ASK FOR OTHERS + YOURSELF.

YIELD TO GOD TODAY. WAIT + LISTEN.

- *Read Isaiah 6:1-10 and write out Isaiah's response in verse 5.*

Ruined! The word leaped out from the page and captivated my heart, while arresting my flesh simultaneously. *Ruined!* Why had I not seen this before? *Ruined!* What did this mean, and how did this one word transform a portion of Scripture I had read many times before? *Ruined!* I could not stop looking at the word "ruined." I tried to turn away and take a deep breath, but God would not let my gaze set anywhere else but upon this word. *Ruined!*

As a young girl I heard Isaiah 6:1-10 preached by various people and interpreted in various ways, but here I was in Bible college, studying in my apartment, when Isaiah 6 caused me to see God differently.

In order to see God as holy, you must be ruined!

I sat a little bit longer and asked God to show me why this moment seemed to parallel the story in Isaiah 6:1-8. Here I was, two years since God called me to preach His Word, and I felt as if I knew nothing at all. I had been serving in a leadership capacity before attending school, and upon my arrival, the Lord asked me to stop a lot of activities I had been doing in ministry. I thought it odd at first, but here in Isaiah, it all made sense.

Like Isaiah, I had been living life one way. I loved God and wanted to serve Him with my whole heart, but unbeknownst to me, my heart was divided. I was unaware of this truth because nothing seemed to be standing in my way. I was obedient when God said, "Go." I prayed faithfully and fasted frequently. I could hear His voice and thought I had been doing a pretty good job in nurturing my relationship with the Father, Son, and the Holy Spirit. I had encountered the Lord in a real way that set my heart ablaze for His Word and for His people.

But what was dividing me? Simply, it was all the other "kings" I had set over my life that were keeping me from seeing God as holy. It was my own father whose approval meant everything to me. It was the desire to be normal, to fit in, and not feel isolated because of the choice I made to completely follow God. It was not moving forward in what I knew God wanted me to do for fear of failure and fear of losing.

It was using my gifts and talents to honor God, not knowing I was to do more than provide a service, but I was to become a servant. Before now, I believed I had a clear view of my Father in Heaven. Now, I had to decide if I would continue to let these things keep me from seeing Him as the angels and Isaiah did after his vision. I slowly dropped to my knees and realized I was now being faced with the reality of my humanity and God's deity. Like Isaiah, all I could say was: *Woe is me! For I am ruined...*

- **Have you ever been in a similar state? What caused you to feel ruined?**

In Isaiah 6:5, the word "ruined" denotes the following: *Damah: to cease, cause to cease, cut off, destroy* (*Strong's Concordance*.1820).

When Isaiah saw the Lord, he encountered Him. To encounter someone means to meet him or her. He was not encountering the Scriptures, nor was he resting on the experience of someone else. Here, he was given total access to see and be seen by the Creator of all. It was in this exchange that Isaiah discovered who he is and who he is not. No longer could Isaiah stand in the presence of God without acknowledging his need to be ruined.

- **Have you ever encountered God in a profound way, a way that changed everything?**

Everything from Isaiah's past had to be cut off. Everything attached to whom he believed God to be had to be destroyed. Every idol and its role in his life had to cease. Why? Because God was going to send him as His mouthpiece. If any residue of former things remained, Isaiah couldn't go in the manner God wanted him to go, which was to be wholly submitted.

Without being ruined, Isaiah could not have been sent.

When looking at God through the eyes of humanity, you miss the beauty of His deity and the splendor of His glory.

I could only imagine what Isaiah felt when seeing this vision unfold. For me, I admitted I did not know God as holy. I rested in what I was previously taught, and a lot of the teachings were limited. I only saw God a few ways, because I only knew God as a few things. He was Provider, Protector, and Healer. But Holy? That was foreign.

Seeing the holiness of God will overwhelm you and cause you to focus on how awesome and big our God really is. Like the angels, our songs of praise should focus on the holiness of God, not only on the things He can do. The word "holy" encompasses all of who God is. It sets Him apart and proves He alone is the only one we need and should desire.

The Father, who sent the Son, who left us with the Holy Spirit, is worthy. When we look to the Son, we know He was ruined for each and every one of us. We celebrate Jesus's death, burial, and resurrection every year during Advent. The day Isaiah was ruined in Isaiah 6:5 was also the day Isaiah was resurrected.

He was willing, just like Jesus, to be sent.

We are ruined for His glory, not our gain!

In 2001, I let God ruin me. That day, in my living room on bended knees, I closed my eyes and saw myself at the feet of Jesus. The only words coming out of my mouth were, "You are holy!" These three little words sent tears down my face. I repeated a second time: "You are holy!" I wanted to say something more, but I couldn't. As I was kneeling there on the floor, I asked God to ruin me.

This sacred space with a sacred God had been carved out for me. What I'd just read in Isaiah was now before me. It is too glorious to describe and too marvelous to leave. After a while, I opened my eyes, and the reality of what had taken place overwhelmed me. I had seen the Lord. The past was behind me. All the kings I built up were now destroyed. My life had been wrecked for the glory of God.

I have never been the same since. The way I live, love, give, speak, share, preach, and write was transformed during that incredible moment. I can say without a shadow of doubt, "My God is HOLY!"

- **Ask God to show you the kings in your life. Write out what needs to be cut off so you can experience God as holy.**

- **Take some time to get on your knees or totally facedown, and imagine yourself before God, and just repeat again and again, "You are holy." Give time and space for the Spirit to ruin you and reveal God's holiness. Record what happened in your time.**

GOD IS HOLY.

Take a moment and write out your own definition for today's attribute of God:

In order to become a doer of the Word, not just a hearer, what can you do today in response to what you have learned about God? (James 1:22)

DOER OF THE WORD

How can you apply what you have learned from the Lord today?

_____
_____
_____
_____

SOCIAL CHALLENGE

// What is something you can share about today?

// Stop and ask God to show you who to share this with today.

// Who should you share this with? (Finish sentence below.)

THIS MESSAGE IS *FOR ALL* BUT IT IS ALSO FOR:

// Pray over that person(s) or group and ask God for an opportunity and courage to share.

IF YOU SHARE ON SOCIAL MEDIA
BE SURE TO USE #SACREDHOLIDAYS + TAG @SACREDHOLIDAYS.

ALL-KNOWING (OMNISCIENT)
by Debra Parker

PRAISE GOD. REPENT OF SIN. ASK FOR OTHERS + YOURSELF.

YIELD TO GOD TODAY. WAIT + LISTEN.

I am sitting in the corner of a coffee shop right now. There are exactly nine people sitting at the tables around me. There are three tables of dark-haired high school students studying for finals, another table surrounded by three generations of beautiful Asian women, and another with a lady sitting alone, organizing her Louis Vuitton purse and wallet. Just outside the window is a Hispanic man in a blue shirt standing at the ATM. A lady in a bright orange shirt just walked up behind him.

And God intimately knows each one.

Earlier today I met Latisha who had amazing, glittered nails. She was the intake person at my doctor's office. I also learned her son recently moved back in with her, she has five grandchildren, and she graduated high school a few years after I was born. She believes there's a purpose behind every encounter she has with someone. After my doctor appointment, I met Sabrina who is a waitress at Le Peep. Then, as I drove to the coffee shop where I now sit, I passed a tall, skinny, male panhandler who hollered at a man in the car next to me—a driver who got out of his car and began throwing punches with the man.

God, in His omniscient power, knows all these people, everything about them—past, present, and future.

- **Read Psalm 139:1-6 and write out what it says about God knowing you.**

The reason I'm telling you about the various people I've noticed today is because I have been asking God to allow me to encounter people as He would—believers and non-believers alike. Take the Samaritan woman; not only did Jesus notice her standing at the well, like any passerby would, He went one step further and desired to connect with her—despite knowing every single thing about her, both the good and the bad. God encourages us to be like Him in this way, that we would encounter people—no matter how flawed—in life-giving, life-changing ways.

You and me . . . we don't want to simply walk by the world we were called to reach. Rather let's visit awhile and love deeply, as God loved us. (John 13:34-35) Am I right?

- *Is your life so busy that you are missing it, especially others? Do you struggle to see, notice, and take time to know others the way God does?*

- *What would happen if we gave people, especially the ones we think don't deserve it, a piece of our heart rather than a piece of our mind?*

Tears are welling up in my eyes now because I realize the more we know and love the people God created, the more we will know and love Him.

Now, back in the coffee shop, an entirely new crew is sitting around me. Directly in front of me are two women with messy topknots. Right now I am envisioning that I am one of those women, and you are the other. If that were the case, I would look into your eyes and remind you: You are known—your past, even the secrets you'd never share, your present, all the ways you feel like you are winning and failing, and your future, with its joys and hardships...every bit of it. You are known and loved.

- *Read Psalm 139:1-18 and make notes about what God knows and what you can know in response.*

- *Now write out, "I am known and loved." Let it sink in, and read it several times, letting its truth settle over your mind and heart. Feel free to make any other notes the Lord impresses on your heart as you take in that truth.*

So go ahead sister, ask in prayer to securely know that you are known. As you go out, remember you take the Spirit, who knows and loves others, with you. This Spirit gives hope, removes darkness, and restores broken hearts.

GOD IS ALL-KNOWING (OMNISCIENT).

Take a moment and write out your own definition for today's attribute of God:

In order to become a doer of the Word, not just a hearer, what can you do today in response to what you have learned about God? (James 1:22)

DOER OF THE WORD

How can you apply what you have learned from the Lord today?

_____
_____
_____
_____

SOCIAL CHALLENGE

// What is something you can share about today?

// Stop and ask God to show you who to share this with today.

// Who should you share this with? (Finish sentence below.)

THIS MESSAGE IS *FOR ALL* BUT IT IS ALSO FOR:

// Pray over that person(s) or group and ask God for an opportunity and courage to share.

IF YOU SHARE ON SOCIAL MEDIA
BE SURE TO USE #SACREDHOLIDAYS + TAG @SACREDHOLIDAYS.

GRACIOUS
by Ashley Irons

PRAISE GOD. REPENT OF SIN. ASK FOR OTHERS + YOURSELF.

YIELD TO GOD TODAY. WAIT + LISTEN.

There's a great woman of faith in Luke 8 who teaches us about grace. Many of you are probably familiar with her story. This woman suffered with an issue of blood for 12 years and spent her entire life searching for healing and relief. She was running out of options when she heard the news of Jesus, the one who heals and restores. She heard of the great things He had done and believed that if only she could touch the hem of His garment, she would receive healing. So she pressed through the crowds, reached out her hand, touching the hem of His garment, and immediately the flow of blood stopped. At which point Jesus says, "Daughter, your faith has made you well."

- *Read Luke 8:40-48. Describe a time you pressed through the "crowds" of doubt, fear, impossibility, or temptation to get near Jesus?*

This woman spent all she had searching for healing, going from doctor to doctor. She was suffering with this sickness and it was only getting worse. By this time, she'd reached her wit's end, which is a good thing, and she was at the right place and at the right time. Jesus, the Healer, was there. Do you notice how she didn't bring anything to Jesus for her healing? Because what Jesus has to offer is not for sale. It's intangible and un-earnable—grace.

- *What kind of healing do you think Jesus was talking about when He said, "Your faith has made you well"? Do you think He was addressing the issue of blood, or the issue of her heart?*

We tend to worry about symptoms more than the real issue of sickness, don't we? Do you think the issue of blood would be her only issue ever in life? No, but the "well" Jesus was referring to was one of salvation. This woman believed when she heard about Jesus, and as a result of her belief, she came to touch His hem. I'd argue that even if the flow of blood hadn't ceased, Jesus would have still let her know that her faith had made her well.

Jesus said, "Go in peace." There was a transaction that occurred, but it wasn't an exchange. She brought nothing, but took everything she needed to sustain her new position and identity in grace. When she touched the hem of His garment, immediately power left Jesus. Do you have that kind of faith? The woman with the issue of blood didn't bring anything, but she took what Jesus gave, and what He gave was power, the same power that would later raise Him from the grave. So she gave nothing, but that power was freely given to her because of her faith, and it was that power that was going to keep her in the position of righteousness, not any work of her own.

- **Read Ephesians 2:8. Because we often forget that it's grace by which we're saved, in what ways do you find yourself "working" to maintain your position as daughter to the King?**

You can't sustain righteousness, but you have power to believe in what Jesus has done for you: He made you righteous. Many of us, after we get saved, somehow forget this principle. Somehow we find ourselves still working to remain righteous. It's like getting a gift we've always wanted, only to get so nervous we might lose it that we barely enjoy it. Then we spend money to protect both the gift and our investments. Have you ever heard of salvation or righteousness insurance? Guess what? You didn't purchase your own salvation or righteousness! Why are you trying to create your own insurance plan for righteousness as if there's anything you could do? You didn't make the investment! Jesus paid it all! So let's pray that He gets what He paid for. So go in peace. Stop toiling. Stop bringing God what He doesn't require of you. Once you've placed your faith in Jesus Christ, which is the greatest gift you could ever receive, there's nothing He requires of us to sustain it.

- **How would your life look different if Jesus stood before you and said, "Go in peace," and you obeyed?**

Jesus tells this woman to go! She didn't need to do any more reaching. She didn't need to touch the hem of His garment again. He said go in peace because the reality is, another hand was about to reach out—His hand. And not just one hand, but both hands stretched-out wide. When He finally reached out, He didn't reach through a crowd, but through death, hell, and the grave. It was His issue of blood that saved us. And when Jesus reached, it was finished. So stop "working" to sustain the gift of grace.

Let me pause here to explain; I want to make sure we're not confusing the process of sanctification for the position of righteousness. Jesus does both the work of positioning us in salvation and righteousness AND the work of sanctifying us—of making us holy. We can get this confused, especially if we know the Bible really well. We can use the Bible as a self-help book, coming up with 10 steps to remain holy. Be careful of subtle legalism. The Bible is not designed as a "how-to" book to become more righteous. It's not a "self-save" book for sanctification. If you think that's the point of the Word, please explain Jesus's reaction to the Pharisees and the scribes. The Bible is reminder that grace is something you can't buy or sustain. All you can do is receive it.

The last words Jesus says to her are "Go in peace, and be healed of your disease." That's weird right? Was she not already healed? Hadn't her faith made her well? What do you think Jesus was talking about? Why would He repeat Himself? Well I didn't know the answers to these question so I decided to focus on the words "well" and "healed," or "whole," and I found they have two completely different meanings. The first mentioning refers to suitability and correctness, and the second mentioning refers to health or disease. By grace through her faith the woman was made righteous or in correct standing with God, and when she touched the hem of Jesus' garment she was made healthy from that one infirmity. So again why would Jesus repeat himself if he already knows these truths? I had to do more digging and I found something I needed to hear. The words "be healed of your disease" referred to a present and continual state of being. Be healed was the woman's new name! When Jesus had called out to see who had touched Him, do you think He didn't actually already know who did? The woman comes to him falling down on the ground in shame and fear. Jesus's last words to her were to let the woman know that she had a new identity that she needed to accept. Be healed, be whole, and exist in freedom because I have set you free from guilt and shame. She was so accustomed to the guilt and shame of her infirmities that she was still addressing the symptoms in a social response. She was being who she had always been.

- **Open your hands now to receive God's gift of grace.**

Jesus gave this woman a new being, and it was beautiful. You know what kind of beauty never fades? Grace. In that moment, in those few words, Jesus robes her in grace, adorns her with freedom, and elevates her identity—and He does this with you. You're beautiful in the eyes of God, but you may need to remind yourself of that fact; it's so easy to forget! Every morning, adorn yourself with it. Robe yourself, bathe in it, brush with it, lace it up, zip it up, tie it up, and carry it on your arms. Whatever you have to do to remind yourself that there's nothing you can do to make God love you anymore and there's nothing you can do to make God love you any less, do it. You can't buy God's grace. You can't sustain God's grace. But you receive God's grace. So adorn yourself in the beauty of it.

GOD IS GRACIOUS.

Take a moment and write out your own definition for today's attribute of God:

In order to become a doer of the Word, not just a hearer, what can you do today in response to what you have learned about God? (James 1:22)

DOER OF THE WORD

How can you apply what you have learned from the Lord today?

_____
_____
_____
_____

SOCIAL CHALLENGE

// **What is something you can share about today?**

// **Stop and ask God to show you who to share this with today.**

// **Who should you share this with? (Finish sentence below.)**

THIS MESSAGE IS *FOR ALL* BUT IT IS ALSO FOR:

// **Pray over that person(s) or group and ask God for an opportunity and courage to share.**

IF YOU SHARE ON SOCIAL MEDIA
BE SURE TO USE #SACREDHOLIDAYS + TAG @SACREDHOLIDAYS.

PROVIDER
by Vivian Mabuni

PRAISE GOD. REPENT OF SIN. ASK FOR OTHERS + YOURSELF.

YIELD TO GOD TODAY. WAIT + LISTEN.

I stood hopping from one foot to the other on the hot sidewalk in front of the mailbox; reading the contents inside the envelope could not wait the fifteen steps to the shaded part of our front porch. With my pointer finger tucked under the seal, I held my breath and ripped open the first envelope. A check for $50 accompanied the response card. Concern grew to panic as I read the note in the second envelope. As missionaries with Campus Crusades for Christ, we live the reality of God as our Provider. We minister in partnership. For 29 years we have relied on donations from churches, individuals, and families for all of the necessary finances to live in order to remain in vocational Christian ministry. The contents of the second letter informed us our $500 a month donor would no longer be supporting us, and only $175 of the needed $10,000 for our summer mission to Japan had come in for our family.

- **Philippians 4:19 says, "And my God will supply every need of yours according to his riches in glory in Christ Jesus." When was the last time you struggled with this promise?**

Once I gathered myself at the mailbox, I ran into the house to show my husband, Darrin, the letter from our ministry partner. And promptly started freaking out. Darrin always remains the calm, steady one in all types of emergencies. Nerves of steel. I am just not wired to be calm—at all. So off I went: "Darrin, our supporters probably hate us because we bought a house! They probably think we have become sucked into the world's system and lost the edge. I can't believe so few of them have responded to our summer missions opportunity. Maybe Japan doesn't seem like a mission field. Maybe we should only do missions in developing nations. Do you think we should've sent two letters? We are supposed to leave in 10 days!"

Meanwhile, Darrin sat in the chair at the dining room table praying, so I joined him. And then I couldn't focus, so I stopped. "Darrin, we could lose our house. I mean, we don't have enough support for the summer, and now losing $500 in monthly donations!"

- **Read Luke 12:22-32. Our provider God tells us not to worry about everyday life; He even provides for ravens and lilies! Reread verse 32. Describe how God feels "to give [us] the kingdom."**

With a clear understanding of God's promises, Darrin looked over at me and calmly said, "Viv, I think the Lord can still provide all we need," and remained confident of God's provision. I, on the other hand, felt frustrated and absolutely desperate. So I decided to fast the entire weekend. Up until then I only fasted for a day at a time or a couple meals at a time. My prayer was simple: "Father, you know how I have a hard time trusting. Would you please bring in at least $1000 of our needed $10,000. If You bring in the $1000, I'll be okay to go to Japan and will trust You with the rest."

- **Read Genesis 22:13-14. When the sacrifice of Isaac, Abraham's son, was averted on the mountain, Abraham called the place, "The Lord Will Provide." Write down the places in your life where you long to see God's provision.**

Monday arrived. The doorbell rang and I peered through the peephole. A man in an official postal uniform stood at our door holding a bin. I threw open the door, eyes wide. He had a bin of mail for us—mail that had been sitting in the post office. I thanked the postal worker, took the large bin, and gently shut our door and slid to the ground. Tears filled my eyes as I looked at all the envelopes.

I started ripping open one after the other: notes of encouragement about moving to our new home, increases to monthly donation amounts, excitement about our summer mission to Japan, and checks totaling over the $1000 I asked the Lord to provide. I was so amazed—"Darrin! Our supporters don't hate us! You were right. God has and will provide."

As I gathered the stacks of junk mail to throw away in the recycling bin, I sensed God speaking—not an audible voice but a very strong impression: "Viv, you think you know how to do this summer missions thing because you've raised support many times: write a letter, include envelopes, add a response card, pray, and run to the mailbox multiple times a day. But I am sending you to a country with less than a one-percent Christian population. You can't just go through the motions. You are engaging in a spiritual battle, and I want your to reliance to be on Me."

- **Philippians 4:19 says, "And my God will meet all your needs according to his glorious riches in Christ Jesus." In confidence that God will meet—supply, accomplish, complete, provide for—all your needs, write a simple prayer of thanksgiving for His provision.**

The entire mail delivery snafu served to wake me from my slumber. I needed to be jolted from going through the motions. I needed fresh faith. God in His kindness and mercy allowed the delivery of only some mail, including the letter about our large monthly donor, to get me desperate enough to pray. And with renewed vision and dependence on God, we took our family and led the team to Japan. God supplied all we needed in the end, and now we look back on our tiny step of faith and celebrate how our first team helped establish a twenty year partnership with Japan that remains to this day.

GOD IS OUR PROVIDER.

Take a moment and write out your own definition for today's attribute of God:

In order to become a doer of the Word, not just a hearer, what can you do today in response to what you have learned about God? (James 1:22)

DOER OF THE WORD

How can you apply what you have learned from the Lord today?

_____
_____
_____
_____

SOCIAL CHALLENGE

// **What is something you can share about today?**

// **Stop and ask God to show you who to share this with today.**

// **Who should you share this with? (Finish sentence below.)**

THIS MESSAGE IS *FOR ALL* BUT IT IS ALSO FOR:

// **Pray over that person(s) or group and ask God for an opportunity and courage to share.**

IF YOU SHARE ON SOCIAL MEDIA
BE SURE TO USE #SACREDHOLIDAYS + TAG @SACREDHOLIDAYS.

PROTECTOR
by Tara Royer Steele

PRAISE GOD. REPENT OF SIN. ASK FOR OTHERS + YOURSELF.

YIELD TO GOD TODAY. WAIT + LISTEN.

I sit here after shedding many tears. I truly did not know this morning would bring what it did. Before dropping the kids off at school, we all talked about daily bread. Bentley was truly worried about something he had going on tomorrow, and I told him, "Son, let's just worry about today. Heck, don't even worry about it, embrace it! God will give you exactly what you need today, your daily bread."

With God's daily bread fresh on my mind, how it protects us from seasons of famine, pain, fear, and confusion, we pulled into the driveway and Rick, my husband, went inside. For some crazy reason I opened an email in the car—and began to sob. It doesn't even matter what it was all about, just know that it stunk and was down right hard—a testing of our faith. I cried out, right there in the car; no one could hear me but God, begging Him for help through bouts of sobbing, snot, and tears. With a huge Red Sea before me, I pleaded for help. Though my flesh couldn't see it, my spirit longed for His protection.

- **Read Exodus 14:13-14. Describe a time you sensed God fighting for you, protecting you from harm.**

I went in the house and found Rick reading the same email. We got on our knees and cried out to Him (cue more snot and bouts of sobbing). See, we don't need to hold it all in. Our tears draw the Lord near, He even "gathers up all [our] tears and puts them in his bottle" (Psalm 56:8). We weren't meant to carry the trials and weight of the world on our shoulders. There are small puddles, ponds, lakes, and Red Seas before us; we just need to be still and cry out to Him. In a way, the tears cleanse our sight so we can see that He will make a way of protection, a way you can't even imagine. So cry harder, friend.

- **Read Psalm 126:5. What circumstance in front of you are you trying to control, trying so hard to be strong against and not cry? Pour it out to Jesus in the space below.**

After falling on our knees, crying tears of God's protection (for tears keep us from holding onto things we need to let go of), He showed up as *Protector* through our friends. Those who speak truth and stand in the gap for us; those who help us see things about ourselves we have a hard time seeing and believing on our own, helping us fight our battles and encouraging us to step out in obedience.

- ***Have you experienced something like this—where a person or a situation was the physical protection of God for you? Reflect on that time below.***

Because of God's protection through every trial, we have persevered and are still alive to tell of His glory, to share our story of His faithfulness. I'm here today, not in the grave, no longer in an abusive relationship, no longer bitter to family, and no longer addicted or lost. He has protected me and carried me with such grace and mercy.

- ***Read 2 Thessalonians 3:3. What does God promise to do?***

Since the email this morning, I've seen glimpses of God's protection and provision, for His daily bread truly is enough. Exodus 23:25 says, "You must serve only the LORD your God. If you do, I will bless you with bread and water, and I will protect you from illness."

What "illness" is compelling you to seek God's protection? Know that He has already provided a path. So, friend, stop fighting with flesh and fight with the eyes of Jesus. He will never leave or forsake you. You just need to be still and let Him fight your battles. His shield is big and He's ready to protect you.

GOD IS OUR PROTECTOR.

Take a moment and write out your own definition for today's attribute of God:

In order to become a doer of the Word, not just a hearer, what can you do today in response to what you have learned about God? (James 1:22)

DOER OF THE WORD

How can you apply what you have learned from the Lord today?

_____
_____
_____
_____

SOCIAL CHALLENGE

// What is something you can share about today?

// Stop and ask God to show you who to share this with today.

// Who should you share this with? (Finish sentence below.)

THIS MESSAGE IS *FOR ALL* BUT IT IS ALSO FOR:

// Pray over that person(s) or group and ask God for an opportunity and courage to share.

IF YOU SHARE ON SOCIAL MEDIA
BE SURE TO USE #SACREDHOLIDAYS + TAG @SACREDHOLIDAYS.

MERCIFUL

by Brooke Saxon-Spencer

PRAISE GOD. REPENT OF SIN. ASK FOR OTHERS + YOURSELF.

YIELD TO GOD TODAY. WAIT + LISTEN.

We often forget that mercy applies to us, not because we think we are wonderful or flawless, but because we convince ourselves that mercy is for others. Though we know we need it, we feel the responsibility to show mercy to others, but not to accept it for ourselves.

What does it mean to be *merciful*? The Merriam-Webster Dictionary defines it this way: "Treating people with kindness and forgiveness: not cruel or harsh: having or showing mercy. Giving relief from suffering." And its variation, *mercy*, is defined as the "kind or forgiving treatment of someone who could be treated harshly. Kindness or help given to people who are in a very bad or desperate situation."

- **When you consider these definitions, what do you envision? Or, whom do you envision?**

I see those who are visibly suffering—those who do not have a home, a bed, a roof over their heads, food to fill their bellies, or clothes to cover their bodies. They may look a little dingy and dirty and, frankly, discarded from the world you and I live in. We may think of these individuals and feel it is our duty to ever so kindly bestow mercy upon them (as if we really even know how to do that), like a king granting a pardon.

Let me suggest another way to envision these definitions. I see us—you and me. We are in a dire situation as well—our souls are dingy and dirty with sin. We may have homes, but they often house our selfishness and greed. We have closets full of clothes, but they act as a veil to our insecurities. We have endless food, but it only fills our own emptiness. And just like the visibly suffering, we too need a pardon.

But when we look beyond the mercy we extend to others and the mercy we realize we need ourselves, we cannot help but come face to face with our merciful God, whose ability to show grace and compassion never ceases, never wavers. According to Psalm 23:6, it's the kind of mercy that follows us all the days of our lives. Notice God's wrath isn't what follows us all the days of our lives, nor is it God's eye-rolling or finger-pointing. Rather, it's His "goodness and mercy." What a kind God we serve!

When King David was in a desperate situation (one of many!), and his guilt was great, he told the prophet Gad, "But let us fall into the hands of the Lord, for His mercy is great. Do not let me fall into human hands" (2 Samuel 24:14). Unlike our ability to show mercy, which lacks consistency due to our pride, insecurities, and biases, God's mercy has no limits and is forever directed our way.

- **Read Hebrews 4:14-16 and write verse 16 below.**

The only place to receive mercy is from Jesus. How beautiful that we are encouraged to come to Him with confidence, not insecurity!

According to the verses we read earlier, and knowing ourselves, our God has every reason to judge us harshly. Instead He chooses mercy—undeserved kindness granted to us!

GOD IS MERCIFUL.

Take a moment and write out your own definition for today's attribute of God:

In order to become a doer of the Word, not just a hearer, what can you do today in response to what you have learned about God? (James 1:22)

DOER OF THE WORD

How can you apply what you have learned from the Lord today?

_____
_____
_____
_____

SOCIAL CHALLENGE

// **What is something you can share about today?**

// **Stop and ask God to show you who to share this with today.**

// **Who should you share this with? (Finish sentence below.)**

THIS MESSAGE IS *FOR ALL* BUT IT IS ALSO FOR:

// **Pray over that person(s) or group and ask God for an opportunity and courage to share.**

IF YOU SHARE ON SOCIAL MEDIA
BE SURE TO USE #SACREDHOLIDAYS + TAG @SACREDHOLIDAYS.

INFINITELY WISE
by Logan Wolfram

PRAISE GOD. REPENT OF SIN. ASK FOR OTHERS + YOURSELF.

YIELD TO GOD TODAY. WAIT + LISTEN.

Truth be told, I have an easier time wrapping my brain around God being all-powerful—one who covers moons in eclipses and both stirs-up and calms seas—than one who is infinitely wise. Because God's glory is evidenced in the world around me, writing about His power and might comes more naturally. Cake.

Trusting in God's infinite wisdom often means that I'll find myself far outside of my ability to understand it. And like most people, I like understanding things.

- ***Is there something going on in your life now, or happened recently, that made you feel very finite (limited) in your wisdom? Explain.***

Life isn't going to make sense. It won't always feel warm and fuzzy and tied-up in a pretty bow. Just because I don't see where it all ends and I can't make sense of everything around me, doesn't make God any less wise or His plan for my life any less good. God's goodness and wisdom isn't dependent upon my "feeling it" in the midst of the challenges I face.

While it may not feel all happy-slappy, somewhere, even in all the not knowing, I find comfort. I can rest in knowing that God's wisdom goes ahead of me and behind. Because the foolishness of God is wiser than human wisdom (1 Corinthians 1:25), I'm confident that my story is laced with the infinite wisdom of an all-powerful God who I can't see, or touch, or oftentimes even feel.

When the Lord brought the people out of Egypt, it says in Exodus 13 that He did not take them the shortest way. The shortest way would take them by the Philistine camp, which would cause fear and a desire to turn back. Rather, God took them the way of the wilderness towards the Red Sea. For their protection, He took them the hard way.

The Lord led His people through the desert with a pillar of cloud by day and fire by night, which was so great because they could see the wisdom of His leading ahead of them. He led them, fed them, and helped them avoid a war zone. Those lucky Israelites never had to wonder if our infinitely wise God was leading them because they could see Him plainly in front of their faces the whole time.

I wish I could see Him plainly in front of me all the time like that.

I wonder, though, how the Israelites felt when their God-cloud led them straight into the banks of a sea with nowhere left to go.

I bet they wondered about His wisdom then too. In fact, I know they did.

- **Write out what Moses had to say to the Israelites in Exodus 14:13.**

Then the pillar of cloud and the angel of God moved from being in front of the Israelites to behind them as Moses parted the Red Sea for Israel to cross on dry land.

Perhaps when we stand firm in the Lord and trust that He is good and powerful and wise, He'll part our seas of insecurity, confusion, pain, and loneliness, leading us to stand on in His infinite wisdom. In that place, we will walk across that which we would have never foreseen in our own finite wisdom.

Maybe when we've come to the end of our ability to understand, we've come to the exact place our infinitely wise God wants us—a place far better than we could have ever dreamed up.

GOD IS INFINITELY WISE.

Take a moment and write out your own definition for today's attribute of God:

In order to become a doer of the Word, not just a hearer, what can you do today in response to what you have learned about God? (James 1:22)

DOER OF THE WORD

How can you apply what you have learned from the Lord today?

SOCIAL CHALLENGE

// **What is something you can share about today?**

// **Stop and ask God to show you who to share this with today.**

// **Who should you share this with? (Finish sentence below.)**

THIS MESSAGE IS *FOR ALL* BUT IT IS ALSO FOR:

// **Pray over that person(s) or group and ask God for an opportunity and courage to share.**

IF YOU SHARE ON SOCIAL MEDIA
BE SURE TO USE #SACREDHOLIDAYS + TAG @SACREDHOLIDAYS.

REFLECTIONS

What have you learned about the character of God this Advent?

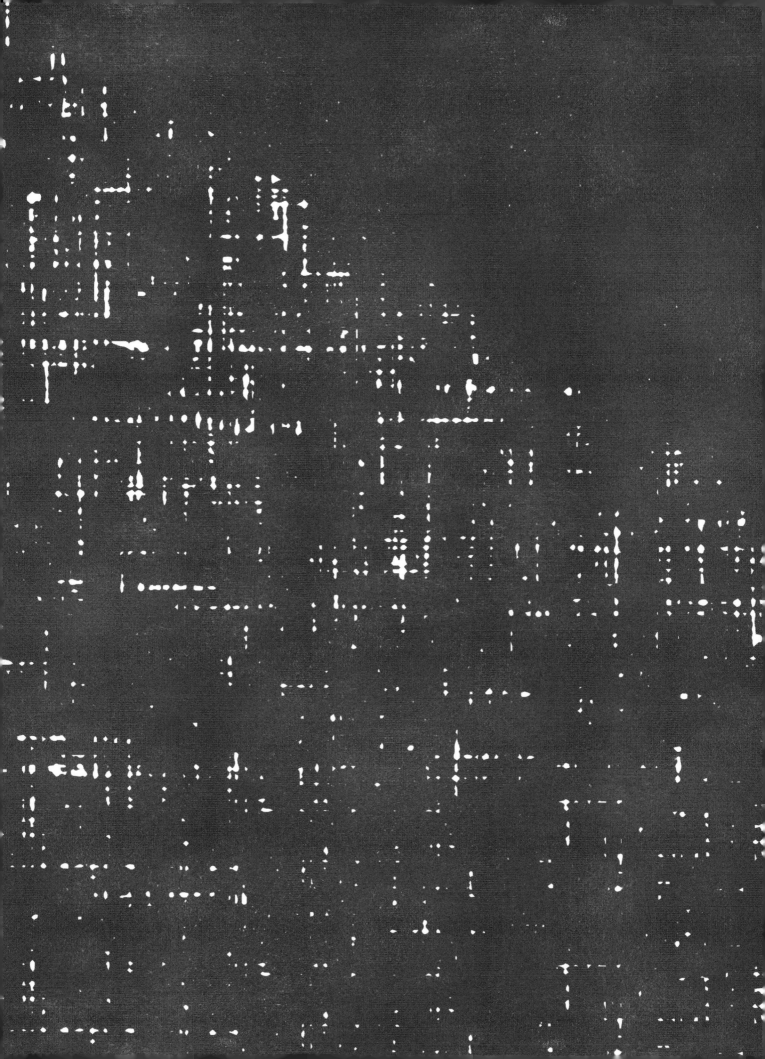

LET'S REALLY STAY FRIENDS

FOR GROUPS AND GROUP LEADERS

We were meant to live in connection and community with others. Let's gather together in groups to encourage, learn, listen, share, laugh, pray, and be women who are for one another during our holidays, and all the ordinary days in between.

Our hope is that we have a group (or more) meeting in each city in the United States. We know this is a crazy time of year for you but this is something that is so worth your time!

For more information on Groups, go to: sacredholidays.com/join-a-group

If you are interested in hosting a group, we think you are so awesome! We have a private Facebook group to support you, plus all kinds of free downloads to help you make your group awesome.

To sign your group up, go to: sacredholidays.com/host-a-group

ABOUT SACRED HOLIDAYS

Sacred Holidays

Helping you find less chaos and more Jesus during the holidays (and all the ordinary days in between).

Bible Studies and Books that bring you more Jesus!

Community through groups, social media, and more.

Resources to equip you for holidays big and small.

Fun, because loving God and others should be lots of fun!

SacredHolidays.com

#sacredholidays | @sacredholidays

Facebook.com/sacredholidays

Facebook.com/groups/SacredHolidaysTribe

BECKY KISER

Founder + CEO of Sacred Holidays and Author of For All

Becky is intent that women would fall in love with God's Word, then feel equipped and empowered to live it out. She believes that women can live out their own wild story, just like the ones we see of God's chosen in His Word, as they love Jesus and love people. She is the founder and CEO of Sacred Holidays—a ministry dedicated to helping women find less chaos and more Jesus during holidays through Bible study, community, resources, and lots of fun! She is determined to help women keep all the whimsy of the holidays, but help make them sacred—holy and set apart. Becky has a background in marketing and ministry and is a certified Myers-Briggs life coach, who brings each of those experiences into her writing and speaking. Becky and her husband, Chris, live in The Woodlands, TX, with their three girls.

Beckykiser.com | @beckykiser | facebook.com/becky.kiser

KELLY BOSCH | GROUP COORDINATOR & ALL THINGS AMAZING

Kelly wholeheartedly believes we are better together. In her mind, life is bolder and brighter when done with others. She is passionate about creating connections through shared experiences and authentic hospitality. Jesus modeled it, and Kelly thinks we should live it out. She gathers people together – whether around a decorated table, over pizza and paper plates, or in a social media group – because she believes every single person deserves to have a seat at the table. We all have a story to tell and she wants to know yours. While around her table, you can expect to hear about her love of story and her fondness for the Marvel Cinematic Universe. She is a lady geek, sports fanatic, adventure seeker, and expert gift giver. Her affection runs deep for smoked brisket, potatoes of any kind, cupcakes, and all things coconut. Kelly lives in the State of Hockey (also known as Minnesota) with her hard-working husband, Jeff, and energetic sons, Xander & Gavin.

@kellynbosch | facebook.com/kellynbosch

MOLLY PARKER | EDITOR

Molly Parker cherishes her role as contributor and editor for both Sacred Holidays and Anchored Press. In addition, she's a contributor for Crosswalk.com, where she weaves God's truth into everyday experiences. She's a toy designer's wife and mother of two teens and a young adult. Having lived in various cities and states, Molly has a heart for folks who miss "home." When she's not french-braiding hair or scolding her basset hound, she's either eating cake, baking a cake, or thinking about cake, which is surprising considering she's worked in the fitness industry 25 years.

@mollyjeanparker | facebook.com/molly.parker.507

MEGAN SJUTS WITH BUILDING 07 | STUDY DESIGNER

Megan Sjuts is the owner of Building 07 and designer for Sacred Holidays. Her mission as a designer is to simplify the design process and serve creative professionals and business owners. Building 07 offers a full range of professional design services that cover the gamut of graphic to web design, and all the creative strategy in between.

When she is not behind the screen designing for clients, she is teaching graphic design courses at Rogue Community College in Southern Oregon, where she lives with her husband, Elliot, their chocolate lab, Dixie, and four chickens, Sunny, Popcorn, Peanut and Penny.

@building07 | Building07.com

MEET THE CONTRIBUTORS

ANDI ANDREW | SURPASSING ORDINARY (TRANSCENDENT)

Andi Andrew has a deep passion to see the fullness of the gospel of Jesus Christ outworked in our everyday lives. Born in Spokane, Washington, and married in Sydney, Australia, she now lives in New York City and is cofounder and copastor of Liberty Church with her husband, Paul. They began Liberty Church in New York City with a heart for cities everywhere, and it now includes local church communities across Manhattan and Brooklyn, as well as St. Petersburg, Florida; San Francisco, California; and Manzini, Swaziland. In 2015, she launched the She Is Free Conference in order to equip and activate women to walk in freedom, strength, and wholeness in spirit, soul, and body. A frequent speaker all over the world and author of She Is Free: Learning the Truth about the Lies That Hold You Captive, and Fake or Follower: Refusing To Settle For a Shallow Faith, she and her husband, Paul, live in Brooklyn with their four children, Ezekiel (Zeke), Jesse, Finley, and Samuel.

andiandrew.com | @andiandrew | facebook.com/andiandrew.page

MEGAN BURNS | HEALER

Megan Burns lives in Minneapolis with her husband, Tom, and their fives kids: Micah, Noah, Stella, Shiloh, and Eliza. She founded She Does Justice in 2012 as an adoption fundraiser and continues to be passionate about empowering women to make a difference in their everyday lives.

@megan.k.burns

CHRISTINE HOOVER | JEALOUS

Christine Hoover is a pastor's wife, mom of three boys, and author of several books, including *Messy Beautiful Friendship* and *Searching for Spring: How God Makes All Things Beautiful in Time*. She podcasts and blogs at Grace Covers Me, where she speaks gospel truths to our honest thoughts. Christine lives with her family in Charlottesville, Virginia.

gracecoversme.com | @christinehoover98 | facebook.com/gracecoversme

ASHLEY IRONS | GRACIOUS

Worship leader, movie buff, event planner, social commentator, music enthusiast, entrepreneur, urban missionary, foodie, learner, and wanna be world traveler; uncommon words for a common girl! Ashley Irons hails from Atlanta, GA but has called Dallas, TX home since 2013. Her passion is to see an authentic, unified Church wisely engaging the world around it. Ashley is praying for a spiritual revival in the American church and is sacrificially pursuing opportunities for it to begin with her. Graduating with a degree from Dallas Theological Seminary, Ashley pursued full-time ministry at her church, Oak Cliff Bible Fellowship, in 2017. In her spare time, Ashley enjoys co-hosting a podcast called We Talk Different, babysitting her godchildren, and collecting recipes on Pinterests.

Wetalkdifferent.com | @ashleyironsdoesthings | @wetalkdifferent

JAMIE IVEY | FAITHFUL

Jamie is a podcaster, writer, and speaker from Austin, Texas. She is the proud mama to four kids and wife to Aaron, worship pastor of The Austin Stone Community Church. Jamie loves to encourage women to passionately follow Jesus through whatever stage of life they might find themselves in. Jamie hosts the popular podcast, The Happy Hour with Jamie Ivey, and her book, If You Only Knew released early in 2018.

Jamieivey.com | @jamieivey | facebook.com/JamieIvey5678

ASHLEY MORGAN JACKSON | GOOD

Ashley Morgan Jackson is a wife, mother, and warrior of the Spirit. Her greatest passion is to see women fall more in love with Jesus, His Word and let Him change them until it encompasses every aspect of their lives. When she's not sharing devotions on Instagram you might find her lifting weights, drinking (another) cup of coffee, having a dance party with her family, or listening to podcasts while she cleans her house.

Ashleymorganjackson.com | @ashley.morgan.jackson | facebook.com/ashleymorganjacksonblog

LEIGH KOHLER | JUST

Leigh Kohler, speaker, writer, teacher and advocate, is co-founder and Executive Director of the Alliance. Her own personal journey in the fight for justice began after being heartbroken while learning about the reality of human trafficking. Leigh is a knowledgeable and passionate speaker for God's mercy and justice. She has spoken to numerous audiences on the issue of human trafficking, including a panel discussion at the Passion Conference in 2013. She loves teaching God's Word and is passionate about seeing people set free – physically and spiritually. She would say that her greatest thrill in all of life has come from knowing Jesus and following Him.

Freedomchurchalliance.org | @leighkohler | @freedomchurchalliance | facebook.com/leigh.kohler

VIVIAN MABUNI | PROVIDER

Vivian is national speaker and writer with a passion to see women and men influence the college campus, families, churches, communities and the world with hope and life found through intimacy with God. Her first book, "Warrior In Pink: A Story of Cancer, Community and the God Who Comforts" (Discovery House Publishers) released in April 2014. Her next book for WaterBrook Multinomah, (a division of Penguin Random House) will release summer of 2019. With 29 years of ministry experience on staff with Cru, Vivian loves teaching about the bible and practical application to ministry and life and is slowly working on her Masters in Bible Exposition at Talbot Seminary. Vivian has written for SheReadsTruth and is a speaker for IF:Gathering. Married 27 years to her husband, Darrin, they live in Mission Viejo, CA with their kids, Jonathan, Michael, and Julia. Vivian loves coffee, shoes, sushi and social media, so stay in touch with her.

Vivianmabuni.com | @vivmabuni | facebook.com/VivianMabuniWriter

SARAH MAE | COMFORTER

Sarah Mae has a past that would be her present if it weren't for Jesus. A blogger, author, and co-author of Desperate: Hope for the Mom Who Needs to Breathe, she's currently writing The Complicated Heart, a book for broken-hearted lovers of Jesus.

Sarahmae.com | @sarahmaewrites | facebook.com/sarahmaewrites

REMI ONAYEMI | RIGHTEOUS

Remi Onayemi is passionate about equipping women to lead a life worthy of their calling. The Lord has been kind in allowing Remi opportunities to teach the truth of God's Word in various parts of the United States as well as in Nigeria, Kenya, Spain and East Asia. Remi received biblical training from the Downline Institute for Women in Memphis, Tennessee in addition to the Kanakuk Institute in Branson, Missouri. Originally from Chicago, Remi spent 6 years working as an educator in the Chicago Public School system and several years thereafter traveling the U.S. in recruitment of gospel-centered believers who are passionate about improving the urban education system in America. Remi holds a Bachelor of Arts degree in Elementary Education from Trinity International University in Deerfield, Illinois and a Master of Arts in Youth and Family Ministry from John Brown University in Siloam Springs, Arkansas. Remi currently serves in the role of Groups Minister for The Village Church in Flower Mound, Texas. In her spare time she greatly enjoys dancing, travel, times of encouraging fellowship with friends, and jumping out of airplanes!

@RemiJoy | facebook.com/remi.onayemi

DEANNA OPHEIM | UNCHANGING (IMMUTABLE)

Encourager of women, truth-teller, wordsmith, wife, and Bible nerd are all accurate depictions of Deanna. But Deanna's true identity is being a Daughter of God! A piece of her mission is to inspire sisters in the Kingdom to walk out their God-given purpose. Throughout the Bible, God uses women to birth restitution, reformation, and revelation. Deanna's calling in ministry is to walk with a union of women similar to this. Deanna attended Texas State University and is currently enrolled in seminary at Austin Graduate School of Theology.

@deannaopheim | facebook.com/dee.brooks1

KATIE ORR | TRUTHFUL (VERACITY OF GOD)

Katie Orr is passionate about helping women enjoy God daily. As a national conference speaker, prolific author, and online coach she provides biblical teaching and relevant resources to help women jump-start their journey toward walking with Jesus. A former Cru college minister, and mother to three, she and pastor-husband, Chris, serve together in the local church.

Katieorr.me | @thekatieorr | facebook.com/thekatieorr

DEBRA PARKER | ALL-KNOWING (OMNISCIENT)

Anywhere Adventurer. Jesus follower. Sometimes burns cookies.

wildfirecollective.tv | @debraparker | @wildfirecollective | facebook.com/heydebraparker

KAI A. PINEDA | HOLY

Kai A. Pineda is a graduate of Rhema Bible Training Center with a degree in Pastoral Leadership and has been married for 9 1/2 years to her (promise from God), second husband Alex Pineda, after becoming a widow in her first marriage. She is the mother of a cute Maltese-Poodle named McLovin, and is trying now to conceive her first child. Before marriage, Kai worked as an Associate/Assistant Pastor, Director of Administration, Worship Leader and Speaker. Now she spends most of her days running the 4 church plants she leads with her husband, cooking three times a day, speaking and singing, and counseling both private clients and couples, all while working on her first book. Her day of rest is every Monday where you will find her watching all her previously recorded shows and binging on documentaries. Wrapped in a blanket with McLovin at her side, she also loves watching Netflix and Hulu on her Firestick TV, working on her iMac, and oftentimes journaling or writing a new song. Kai still travels extensively throughout the year, but makes sure home is taken care of first.

Kaipineda.com | @kai_a_pineda | facebook.com/kai.a.pineda

BROOKE SAXON-SPENCER | MERCIFUL

Brooke Saxon-Spencer is the founder and editor of Belong Magazine, a quarterly digital and print magazine celebrating the art and community of blogging, social media and entrepreneurship. Brooke is an introvert, Starbucks addict, M&M fiend, wife to her college sweetheart, mother of three, work-from-homer, midwestern girl at heart living in SoCal, and super multi-tasker. She founded Belong Magazine out of her desire for community--a desire to encourage women to use their voices and be confident in their value, a hope for women to use the screen in front of them to connect beyond that screen, to discover "their place" and find "their people". She hopes Belong will serve as a map directing women to one another, connecting them in life-giving ways.

Belong-mag.com | @belongmag | facebook.com/belongmag

TARA ROYER STEELE | PROTECTOR

i'm tara royer steele. i live in brenham, texas, but at times i feel i live in round top, texas. i love our heavenly father and fall in love with him more and more everyday. he amazes me with his love, mercy, kindness and grace. he pours out abundantly. i'm married to rick steele, he's my best friend, my business partner in everything and he leads so well. we have two boys, brayden and bentley! they are joy. joy. joy. they are straight up boys. dirt, baseballs, dirt, footballs, video games and full of snuggles for their momma. i grew up in our family business, royers round top cafe. together we have royers pie haven & two sparrows roasting company in round top, texas. they are businesses built around a place to rest, great food, drink & relationships. we also have, the brave gathering, our favorite. we hold yearly camps for men and women to gather, rest, to strip back the layers added by the earthly world and get back to who they were originally created to be. we hold the camps at amazing venues throughout round top, but recently bought 7 acres to host camps. over the last 31 years in round top, i have gone through hard things & when i truly began to KNOW & understand God and his plan, there was a shift in everything. i was able to learn from my life experiences and share them with others. i love to meet people right where they are & just love.

Graceupongracegirl.com | @graceupongracegirl | facebook.com/tara.r.steele

LISA WHITTLE | ALL-POWERFUL (OMNIPOTENCE)

Jesus is everything. It is the heart, the passion and the leadership approach of author and speaker, Lisa Whittle. Lisa is the author of 6 books including her latest, Put Your Warrior Boots On, and host of the 5 Word Prayers Daily podcast, a popular daily 5-minute power punch of inspiration. She's a sought out Bible teacher for her wit and bold, bottom line approach. Wife, mom, lover of laughter, good food and The Bible, Lisa is a grateful work in progress.

Lisawhittle.com | @lisawhittle | facebook.com/lisawhittleofficial

MARY WILEY | ETERNAL

Mary Wiley works in Christian publishing and hosts the Questions Kids Ask podcast. She is passionate about helping women better understand and love Scripture so that they may be pointed to worship Him more deeply. Mary holds a BA in Theology and English and is currently pursuing a Masters of Arts in Theological studies. She lives in Nashville with her two toddlers and sweet husband and loves adoption, coffee, chips and guac, and lazy Saturdays.

Marycwiley.com | @marycwiley | facebook.com/QuestionsKidsAsk

LOGAN WOLFRAM | INFINITELY WISE

Logan Wolfram would give you full access to her pantry if you lived next door. She is a plate-juggling mom, wife, creative, speaker, and the author of Curious Faith; Rediscovering Hope in the God of Possibility. It is her heart's desire to see women thrive in their relationships with Christ and those around them. Along with her husband, Jeremy, she divides most of her time wrangling two growing boys, three dogs, and a household that magically multiplies dirty laundry. They reside in Greenville, South Carolina which she thinks is pretty much the perfect city.

loganwolfram.com | @LoganLWolfram | facebook.com/LoganLWolfram

ELIZABETH WOODSON | SOVEREIGN

Elizabeth Woodson is a passionate bible teacher whose deepest desire is to know Christ and to make him known! Engaging both the heart and mind she loves to teach the truth of Scripture, empowering believers to experience abundant life with Jesus. Whether it's over a cup of coffee or a few of scoops of ice cream, Elizabeth also loves to disciple women. She believes in keepin' it real as she strives to encourage them to be mighty women of God!

@missjazzyliz | facebook.com/lizwoodson

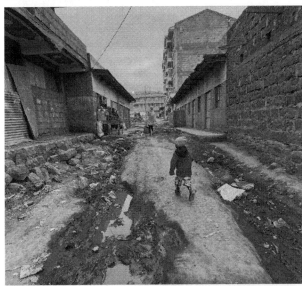
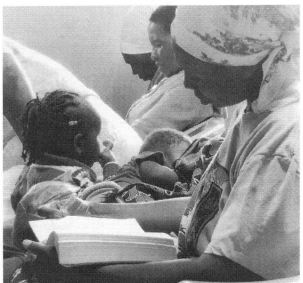

10% FOR VULNERABLE WOMEN AND CHILDREN IN KENYA (LEARN MORE!)
OUR PARTNERSHIP WITH HIS VOICE GLOBAL

His Voice Global (HVG) is called to work in areas of the world with high populations of vulnerable women and children to partner with local leaders to fulfill their vision to care for, educate, and encourage the vulnerable women and children in their area. We currently have partnerships in South Sudan, Kenya and Uganda.

Sacred Holidays specifically partners with our work in Kenya. HVG works in a city in which prostitution and the commercial sex trade industry dominates the economy. Women and children, both by force and by choice, work the streets in order to feed and house themselves and their children. We are partnered with a local Kenyan church called Rift Valley Fellowship (RVF). RVF staff works tirelessly to help these women and children get off the streets and into affordable homes and integrity filled jobs. We have a boys and a girls home, providing holistic restoration including safety, education, counseling, and over all physical care. As children come into our care, we work closely with their mothers through a ministry to the women called Women of Courage. Women of Courage exist to love, provide, disciple, and train women in trades that they can eventually support themselves.

HOW YOU CAN HELP!

First, you already have! You purchasing this study has provided funds for this work!

- ☐ If you'd like to do more, there are so many ways you can help advocate for these beautiful women and children in Kenya.

- ☐ Educate yourself. Hear the stories and the needs. Follow His Voice Global on social media: @hisvoiceglobal and facebook.com/hisvoice. Also, learn lots more and sign up for our newsletter so that you can grow as an advocate for these vulnerable women and children in Kenya at www.hisvoiceglobal.com

- ☐ Support a child by giving them an education: For an Elementary and Middle School study it is $165 a year, or just $14 a month. For High School students it's $600 a year, or $50 a month. This sacrifice on your part is what will change the future of that kids life!

- ☐ Support a mother as she chooses to stay off the streets: $135 a month to provide a home, food, hygiene items, clothing, and job support.

- ☐ Provide a week worth of food for our feeding program that keeps kids from working the street in order to eat. It also pays to feeds everyone in the Recovery program on Saturdays and anyone who comes to church on Sunday, often their only meal/meals of the weekend. $170 a week. We know this is a larger expense, so grab a few friends and go into this together if this isn't something you could do on your own.

- ☐ Sign up to go to Kenya or Uganda with our teams! Contact amber@hisvoiceglobal.com for more information on our trips.

- ☐ Become a monthly partner of His Voice Global! There are countless needs to come up to support the work being done in Kenya. By giving generally you allow there to be resources for the local church to meet the needs of the people as they arise.

- ☐ Host an advocacy night in your home. Grab 10 or so (or more!) of your friends and host a night in your home where they can learn about His Voice Global. We will provide you with video or a staff member to come and share. This can look any way you want it! You can have it low key or super to-do! During the halftime of a big game, or an entire dinner and program. Contact amber@hisvoiceglobal.com and she will make it happen! We can brainstorm together what would be the most fun and best fit for your people.

P.S. from Becky

Ladies, I cannot encourage you enough to do something, anything. I endorse very few ministries because I want you to know the things I push you to be a part of are worth your time, doing real work, and being good stewards of your funds. I have been to Kenya now twice and have known Amber and Vernon, the founders of this ministry for nearly two decades—they and this ministry are the real deal. I have stood in the homes of women who were once prostituting themselves all throughout the day just to provide a bite to eat for the week for their family. But God. He has used HVG and RVF to bring about His redemption story.

FOLLOW HIS VOICE GLOBAL ON SOCIAL MEDIA!

Instagram: @hisvoiceglobal | Facebook: His Voice Global

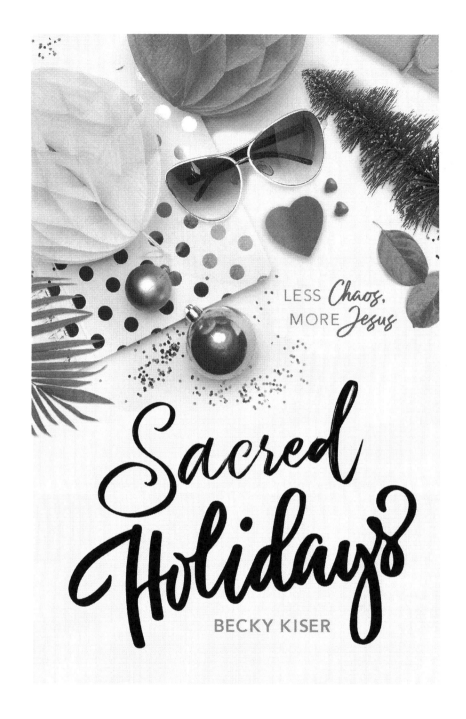

EXCERPT FROM SACRED HOLIDAYS: LESS CHAOS, MORE JESUS BY BECKY KISER

Available where books are sold online:

Copyright © 2018 by Becky Kiser
All rights reserved.
Printed in the United States of America

978-1-5359-1412-3

Published by B&H Publishing Group
Nashville, Tennessee

Dewey Decimal Classification: 394.2
Subject Heading: HOLIDAYS \ STRESS (PSYCHOLOGY) \
FAMILY TRADITIONS

Published in association with D.C. Jacobson & Associates, LLC, an Author Management Company, www. dcjacobson.com.

Unless otherwise noted, Scripture is taken from the English Standard Version. ESV® Text Edition: 2016. Copyright © 2001 by Crossway Bibles, a publishing ministry of Good News Publishers.

Also used: *The Message* (MSG), copyright © 1993, 1994, 1995, 1996, 2000, 2001, 2002 by Eugene H. Peterson

Also used: New Living Translation (NLT), copyright © 1996, 2004, 2015 by Tyndale House Foundation. Used by permission of Tyndale House Publishers, Inc., Carol Stream, Illinois 60188. All rights reserved.

Also used: New International Version®, NIV® Copyright ©1973, 1978, 1984, 2011 by Biblica, Inc.® Used by permission. All rights reserved worldwide.

Cover design by Studio Nth.
Author photo © Amanda Liberto.

1 2 3 4 5 6 7 • 21 20 19 18

CONTENTS

How to Use This Book *(because it's different than other books you've read)* 1

PART 1: LESS CHAOS, MORE JESUS (READ NOW)

Chapter 1 | Regrets, Better Ways, and Baby Steps 13
Chapter 2 | Social Experiments and All Things Whimsy 27

PART 2: HOLIDAYS (READ 30–60 DAYS BEFORE HOLIDAY)

Chapter 3 | New Year's 39
Chapter 4 | Valentine's Day 57
Chapter 5 | Lent and Easter 69
Chapter 6 | Summer 85
Chapter 7 | Halloween 101
Chapter 8 | Thanksgiving 115
Chapter 9 | Advent and Christmas 125
Chapter 10 | Happy Birthday 147

PART 3: COMMON STRUGGLES (READ AS NEEDED)

Chapter 11 | How to Not Be *THAT* Christian 159
Chapter 12 | Realistic Expectations 171
Chapter 13 | Conflict, Drama, and All the Feels 181
Chapter 14 | Budgets and Generosity 197
Chapter 15 | Schedules and Plans 209
Chapter 16 | Grief 217
Chapter 17 | Santa and the Easter Bunny 229
Chapter 18 | P.S.: Be Yourself and Be with Others 237

Acknowledgments 239

HOW TO USE THIS BOOK

BECAUSE IT'S DIFFERENT THAN OTHER BOOKS YOU'VE READ

Holidays can be crazy. And because you're holding this book in your hands, I think you'd agree. I love that about you—you are willing to face crazy head-on and do something about it. Holidays can be especially tricky to navigate as a Christian—wanting to celebrate and focus on Christ yet being pulled into the chaos or whimsy of each holiday.

You aren't alone; nearly every woman I talk to struggles with this. You don't have to stay in the same cycle of wishing things would be different. Jesus called us to not just live, but to live abundantly (John 10:10). This is the beginning of a new way of doing holidays—one that involves less chaos, more Jesus, and not getting too caught up in the holiday whimsy or magical festivities, nor overwhelmed by the holiday chaos.

I am so proud of you for getting this book! You're about to begin a journey to making holidays more sacred—holy and set apart! This book is laid out a little different than most books you've read before, so I wanted to walk you through how to use it.

WHAT THIS BOOK MEANS BY "SACRED"

Throughout this book, you'll hear me say a phrase over and over: "sacred—holy and set apart." Before we go any further, let me tell you what I mean by that phrase. I'm breaking up your approach to the holidays into two categories.

First, *holy*. I want to help your holidays become holy or *dedicated* to Christ (and others). Instead of getting lost in the way the culture does holidays (making it all about self or about applause you could receive for pulling off a perfect event), I want us to get lost in the reality that Christ gave us these holidays to enjoy, and that we can worship Him in the middle of all the whimsy. Even if a holiday isn't a direct celebration of Christ Himself, we can still put Christ and others at the center of all our celebratory moments instead of ourselves! While we don't want to over-spiritualize every single moment, sometimes we can be guilty of under-spiritualizing, can't we? Part of my mission in this book is to help you find more Jesus in each holiday, making it more holy for you, your family, and your friends.

Second, *set apart*. While we certainly want to make the holidays more about Jesus, we don't have to believe the lie that spiritual means impractical. Sometimes we need help setting apart a holiday from the rest of the calendar year, making it special with intentional planning. The "set apart" portion of the holiday chapters are simply there to help you be more intentional about your holiday habits in really practical ways.

As you'll see in each of the chapters that deal with specific holidays, I give you ideas about both of these categories. If you struggle with following in the culture's footsteps and forgetting the spiritual side of the holidays, lost in a sea of Pinterest activities and exhaustion, you'll see some ideas on how to make your holiday more holy, helping you get more Jesus! On the flip side, if you struggle with over-spiritualizing the holidays to the point of never even getting to practical ways of having fun, you'll also see some fun ideas on how to make your holiday "set apart" from the mundane of everyday life with whimsical activities and intentional plans. Sometimes during the crazy of celebration seasons, we need to pull away for more Jesus. Other times we need to bust out the planner, take the bull by the horns, and get intentional about our holiday planning so that we can look back and say it was truly set apart from the rest of the year in practical and fun ways. This book doesn't make you choose; it will help you make your holidays more holy *and* set apart.

THIS BOOK IS MEANT TO STAY OUT

I don't mean stays out in that pile of books you hope to read that crowd up your nightstand, taunting you from your shelves, unread. This book is one you keep within easy reach because you will want to reference it throughout the year. This book of yours is meant to be a companion that guides you through all holidays—not just the big ones. If we can change how we approach the holidays, our lives will be so much more free and full—and headed toward abundant living!

This past year I started keeping my planner on the counter, opened to the current day. By placing my planner out where I could see it each day, it radically changed my perspective on all the things I was juggling. I felt less overwhelmed and more in control than ever. I approached life with more intention and reached more goals than I ever could have imagined. I was able to say no to more things because I was able to see that I simply could not make them fit. I became a better follower of Jesus, wife, mom, friend, teacher, writer, boss, and neighbor. Don't get me wrong, I still have a long way to go. But this simple step of putting my planner out was a game changer.

What if you did the same thing with your holidays? What if instead of waiting to think about them right before they happen, or regretting afterward that you didn't approach them with more intention, you were prepared a month or two in advance? Let's stop living life in survival mode, constantly on the defense, a victim of our schedules and the expectations of others. Instead, let's live sacred—holy and set apart—with our holidays having less chaos, and more Jesus.

THIS BOOK IS MEANT TO BE READ IN STAGES

This book is broken up into three sections:

PART 1: LESS CHAOS, MORE JESUS

(READ RIGHT AWAY)

I know you want to quickly get to the meat of this book, the holiday chapters, where you'll receive practical insights for how you can make your holidays sacred. However, we must deal with our heart and our approach to holidays first. This section is to help set the stage for what it truly means to have less chaos and more Jesus during the holidays. Make time to read these two chapters before you begin the holiday chapters.

Before we get busy "doing," I want to remind you about the story of Mary and Martha in Luke 10. I think sometimes Martha gets a bad rap from her interaction with Jesus inside her home. Oftentimes she is portrayed as this frantic, bitter, workaholic woman, and the truth is, we just don't know that about her character. Sometimes I wonder if she was just like you and me—simply wanting to serve others and Jesus. Like her, we want to create this culture and way of life that brings God glory and others lots of joy. However—and this is a big however—we get lost in our doing and we just need to stop. Mary stopped and was found simply sitting at Jesus' feet, listening to what He had to say. Then we learn the real problem with Martha wasn't that she was serving but that she was *distracted* in her serving (v. 40). Jesus replied in verses 41–42, "Martha, Martha, you are anxious and troubled about many things, but one thing is necessary. Mary has chosen the good portion, which will not be taken away from her."

In Part 1 we will focus on the good portion before we focus on the tasks of carrying things out. Obviously, Martha had to work or else no one would eat. The problem wasn't in her working; it was in being so distracted she missed the good portion. Let's not miss it by being so distracted in our attempts to make holidays sacred. Let's first sit, listen, and learn. Then we can set the table and make the meal, but let's not be distracted by those first.

PART 2: HOLIDAYS

(READ 30–60 DAYS BEFORE HOLIDAYS)

You can certainly read Part 2 right away, but 30–60 days prior to each holiday, refer back to this section in order to receive the most continual benefit. Here you will find the following in each chapter:

- Encouragement in living sacred during this holiday.
- A little historical—cultural and/or religious—context.
- Write your personal mission statement or hope for that holiday.
- Ideas for all women to live sacred during each holiday.
- Ideas for the kiddos in our lives to live sacred too. *(Note: this isn't just for moms; see the section below to be reminded that this book is for every type of person, single, married, with kids, or otherwise, not just parents!)*
- Journaling space for you to record what's worked and what hasn't worked.
- Journaling space for you to record any ideas you can try in the future.

Go ahead and schedule your alerts on your calendar to prepare for each holiday. Set them as an annual recurring event. If you aren't able to make that appointment to plan, then commit to reschedule it for a better time. Since you are scheduling your holiday prep-time a year or more in advance, you will have to make adjustments. However, a simple reminder will increase the chances that you will make the time to sit down.

Check the box below after you've put the session on your calendar for each holiday:

- ❏ New Year's (schedule in November or December)
- ❏ Valentine's Day (Schedule in December or January)
- ❏ Lent and Easter (Schedule in January or February)
- ❏ Summer (Schedule in April or May)
- ❏ Halloween (Schedule in August or September)
- ❏ Thanksgiving (Schedule September or October)
- ❏ Advent and Christmas (Schedule in October or November)
- ❏ Happy Birthday (Schedule in _____)

PART 3: COMMON STRUGGLES

(READ AS NEEDED)

Finally, decide which common struggles you would benefit from reading. You might find it helpful to read through each of those chapters now, so you've learned what they have to teach you. Then come back to them as a refresher before the holidays hit. Know that your needs for each of these chapters will change year after year, hence the reason to keep this book within easy reach at all times.

THIS BOOKS IS MEANT TO GET MESSY

This resource was written for interaction. I view it as part book/part resource, in hopes that you no longer have to search the Internet for hours and hours to try to find what may or may not work for you. I have included some of the best practices for holidays—both the internal processing and prep that you'll find in Part 1 and in each of the holiday chapters from Part 2. However, there are many opportunities for you to process things out in this book. I will give you prompts and ask you questions, providing space for you to answer. Use this space; don't keep your pages clean. The more you interact with this book and make it your resource, the more sacred—holy and set apart—your holidays will become.

I have a sign that hangs at the bottom of my stairs that reads, "Pardon the mess but my children are making memories." I have it hanging there as a joke for others to read before they enter the war zone that can be our upstairs family room and my girls' shared bedroom. No matter how hard we try to clean or how many chore charts I hang, that space is always a mess. That sign reminds me each time I go upstairs that the messes are memories that my girls are making. I don't want them to live in a home with plastic coverings over our furniture or dishes they are afraid to touch. I want them to live in our home and make a ton of memories in it.

I have the same hope for you, my friend. This book is yours and I want you to make a mess with it. The more messes you make in it, the more memories you will have.

THIS BOOK IS MEANT FOR EVERYONE (NOT JUST PARENTS!)

I was very hesitant to include ideas for kids in this book for two reasons. First, I didn't want any person who wasn't a parent to feel like this book wasn't for them. It is so for you! It is for every person. The truth is, most of us have kids in our lives in some capacity—we are aunts, teachers, volunteers, grandparents, friends with moms, etc. These ideas I list are for anyone with a kid in their life, which is pretty much anyone! The hope is that we will all find ways to help train up children to have a more sacred approach to the holidays.

Second, I do not want parents to make holidays all about their kids. This is probably the number one question I get with Sacred Holidays, the ministry: "How can I help my kids learn more about Jesus during the holidays?" I love the heart of these parents so much, and I so get it. And as a ministry leader, I know I could be far more "successful" if I were to monopolize on this desire. The problem is, even though the intent is beautiful, the approach can be imbalanced. The best analogy I have for this is how the flight attendant says that we must first put our oxygen masks on and then help the child. For our children to have the best chance at life, we must first take care of ourselves. This is hard for us as moms because we will do just about anything for our kids. However, and this is a really big however, our goal is not to raise little Christian robots; our aim is to make disciples of Christ. But every disciple needs a discipler, someone showing them the way, not just telling them what to do (or programming their robot to do the right thing). We must show our kids the way by living the sacred way ourselves.

This book is a timeless resource for you, regardless of what season of life you find yourself.

THIS BOOK IS MEANT TO BE EXPERIENCED ALONGSIDE OTHERS

We can't force others to change their approach to holidays, and that is never our aim. However, we can invite others on the journey toward making our holidays sacred—holy and set apart. The truth is, most of your friends and family members want the same thing you do! They want less chaos. And if they are believers, they want more Jesus too! If they are not, they probably do want the abundant life Jesus could offer through the holidays, but they simply have been searching for solutions in the wrong places. Christian or not, they all want to feel like they are living abundantly during the holidays, not caught up in the whimsy and survival-mode-crazy of it. So let's invite them to join us.

We know that we do better when we do things with others—there is power in numbers. It's the reason why weight-loss programs and workout places that promote group gatherings and accountability models are so successful. When we have others who are trying to make the same kind of changes we are, we do better.

We learn from their ways—what has worked and not worked. We have accountability to follow through. We discover more fun or efficient ways of doing things. We hear "me too" instead of assuming we're the only ones struggling with something. Plus, it's just a whole lot more fun!

Who are some people you could invite on this journey with you?

Send them a text message telling them what you are doing and invite them to join you! Put a check next to their name or cross it off once you've reached out to them.

Also, be sure to check out the Sacred Holidays website (sacredholidays.com) for other ways to build connection and community with our tribe of people, plus our team.

ARE YOU READY?

Okay, let's do this! Let's find less chaos and more Jesus in the holidays ahead! Let's make your holidays more sacred—holy and set apart. And let's find some freedom from common struggles that get the best of us too often.

We'd love to hear from you if you're on board, so we can follow along with your journey and our whole tribe can learn from you (our own virtual group). As you learn things or try things, be sure to tag @sacredholidays and use #sacredholidays in your posts, so we can all learn from and celebrate with one another. We are in this together!

PART 1

LESS *Chaos,* MORE *Jesus*

(READ NOW)

| CHAPTER 1 |

REGRETS, BETTER WAYS, AND BABY STEPS

This is the beginning of a new way for you—a new season of making holidays more sacred—holy and set apart. You should be really proud of yourself that you are taking the time to learn about this and actually making some changes. It's worth it; I can promise you that right now. This will not be easy, but, friend, it is so worth it and you can do this.

How many times have we talked to older women and heard, "I wish I would've done or known that when I was your age"? Let's learn from the women who are ahead of us and choose a different way, the one they wish they would've chosen (the one that still isn't too late for you, if you would consider yourself to be the older woman). We can choose this way when we are twenty-two, thirty-six, forty-four, fifty-nine, sixty-seven, and older. We are never too old for this! Let's not live a life of wishing we would've done something. Starting today, let's live the life we were meant to live—free from regrets and taking one baby step at a time toward a better way!

Holidays have become this imbalanced juxtaposition of chaos and whimsy. We are stressed by the shopping and thrilled by the look on the faces of the ones we spoiled. We are exhausted by the parties yet so excited to get all dressed up to celebrate the day or the person. We are easily irritated by our families and absolutely smitten at the same time. We hate ourselves for eating more than we should yet cannot get enough home cooking and treats. And we're torn between our love for all things whimsical and our deep desire to celebrate Jesus in each of the holidays.

The last one is the hardest, wouldn't you agree? We love Jesus and want to follow Him, yet we struggle to make the holidays about Him. We are stuck doing things the way they've always been done. We are stuck celebrating just as the world celebrates. We are stuck celebrating the way our family has always done it before or the way picture-perfect posts on social media have told us to over the years. The idea of something new, even something sacred, feels a bit overwhelming.

REGRETS

We all have regrets when it comes to the holidays, and oftentimes it's the shame of these regrets that keeps us from thinking we are even capable of a better way.

My biggest regret during all the holidays is how I inevitably default to the thirteen-year-old version of myself. When it was New Year's, I used to set big (and unrealistic) goals for myself, resolutions that lasted all of a week. On Valentine's Day, I was more concerned about who was showing me love than loving others (and chocolate, really it's about the chocolate). During Easter, it seemed to be more about the dress (priorities!). Summer can be a whirl of trying to have as much fun as possible. Halloween feels like a slightly rebellious thing to participate in as a Christian. Thanksgiving is the physical proof I turned thirteen when I'm surrounded by every member of my family. Christmas, while a celebration of Jesus' coming, can easily be overshadowed by wish lists and events. And my birthday never quite seems to measure up to the expectation in my head.

I'm a mess. We all are. We feel like we should have it all figured out by now and don't understand why we don't.

What Regrets Surround These Holidays?

Ask your Father to remind you of holiday-related regrets. Give yourself time to really process this today. Then, remember that this is your book, your resource for years and years to come. So come back to this page each year and you can add to the list below. The reason why we want to name the regrets is because we want to clearly and specifically identify the things we do not want to continue. There is no shame in naming it. (Tip: be general only when it's referring to someone else. Sometimes it's best to just use the first letter of a name or a place, to keep this page confidential.)

NEW YEAR'S:

_____

_____

VALENTINE'S DAY:

_____

_____

LENT AND EASTER:

_____

_____

SUMMER:

_____

_____

HALLOWEEN:

_____

_____

THANKSGIVING:

_____

_____

ADVENT AND CHRISTMAS:

_____

_____

HAPPY BIRTHDAY (INCLUDING YOUR BIRTHDAY AND OTHERS):

_____

_____

BETTER WAYS

We women are masters at staying in shame longer than we should, but shame has never been ours to carry. I'm a total word nerd and absolutely love the dictionary (and translation dictionaries). *Merriam-Webster's* dictionary defines shame as "a painful emotion caused by consciousness of guilt, shortcoming, or impropriety. A condition of humiliating disgrace or disrepute. Something that brings censure or reproach; something to be regretted."

We just made a long list of regrets, which can tempt us to fall right back into that trap of shame, leading to guilt. We are vastly aware of our shortcomings. Holidays are so sweet and so magical in so many contexts, but we have so many regrets. So we settle into shame and believe there is no better way.

Before we move on to a better way of approaching the holidays, we must clearly identify what is true and what is a lie. What is true is all the things you listed above. We all have regrets about past holidays—wishing that certain elements were different. Identifying each one helps us learn. But the lie becomes evident when we take on shame, which isn't from your Father in heaven. John 8:44 speaks into this concept, "He [the devil] was a murderer from the beginning, and does not stand in the truth, because there is no truth in him. When he lies, he speaks out of his character, for he is a liar and the father of lies."

The father of lies, Satan, slithers right up next to the list of regrets we just processed and tells you, "Things will never change." He leads you to believe you will never get this right. He reminds you of others who have it all together (at least on their social media feed) and puts you in your place. He even tells you what a failure you are for not worshiping Jesus more during the holidays—holidays that are supposed to be about Him. He is the one who puts fear in us around holidays like Halloween or Christmas, causing more fear of the world than a love for others. Being a follower of Jesus in this day is so very complicated, and the enemy is taking every opportunity to slither up next to us and whisper lies in our ears, just as he did to Eve in the garden (Gen. 3).

When we look at our list of regrets above, we can listen to one of two voices: the voice of truth or the voice of lies. Jesus said in John 10:10, "The thief comes only to steal and kill and destroy. I come that they may have life and have it abundantly." I love how *The Message* translation by Eugene Peterson words this verse, "I came so they can have real and eternal life, more and better life than they ever dreamed of."

Yes! Isn't this what you want, my friend? Isn't this why you picked up this book? You believe there is a better way. You believe there must be a way "more and better than you ever dreamed of."

A New and Better Way

Just as we listed our regrets about the holidays, I want you to make a new and "better way" list. This list depicts what could be—and dreams about what you wish and hope would happen during the holidays. Don't over-spiritualize this either. Keep the traditions and cultural whimsy that are good and life-giving. Then ask your Father what might be a better way.

NEW YEAR'S:

_____

_____

VALENTINE'S DAY:

_____

_____

LENT AND EASTER:

_____

_____

SUMMER:

_____

_____

HALLOWEEN:

_____

_____

THANKSGIVING:

_____

_____

ADVENT AND CHRISTMAS:

_____

_____

HAPPY BIRTHDAY (INCLUDING YOUR BIRTHDAY AND OTHERS):

_____

_____

I wish I could sit across from you now and hear these dreams God is creating in you. I know our tendency is to buffer our dreams just in case they don't come about. Here is what I want to encourage you to do, sweet friend: dream without the safety net. Abundant life in Jesus, as we defined earlier, is "more and better than they (that's you!) ever dreamed."

One of my favorite verses in all the Scriptures is the reality check that He is God and we are not, that is found in Isaiah 55:8–9, "For my thoughts are not your thoughts, neither are your ways my ways, declares the Lord. For as the heavens are higher than the earth, so are my ways higher than your ways and my thoughts your thoughts." Our Father takes such delight in our dreams and our faith. The reason why I love dreaming and planning is because it's part of the first steps of faith; it's our acknowledgment that there is actually a better way.

Then our Father takes it from there. He took Noah's first step and used him to build an ark. He took Moses—yes, the fearful-and-afraid-to-speak Moses—and used him to free the Israelites and part an entire sea. He used Esther, from the least favored lineage, to change a king's mind and save her people. He used David, the smallest of all his brothers, to kill the giant Goliath and become a king after God's own heart. He used John, a common fisherman, to be His most beloved disciple and be an elder to the early church for decades. He used Paul, a former persecutor and murderer of Christians, to be a major leader for the first followers of Jesus and writer of much of the New Testament letters.

We invite God into the dreams we hold in open hands, as we walk into each of these holidays asking and expecting Him to bring about a better way—one that is so much greater than anything we could ever imagine. We take the first steps, and He leads the path.

BABY STEPS

As I talk to women about making holidays sacred, I see it in their eyes: to change course feels so very overwhelming. Where do you even start? You start in one place and you pick one thing.

I'm an extremist, so I really struggle with this whole baby-step concept. I'm that person who is either 5 percent or 155 percent in. My closest friends and family know to never play a practical joke on me because I don't know how to respond without taking my reciprocal practical joke too far. It's one of the biggest pet peeves about myself, and most hilarious quirks. I have a really hard time with the whole "slow and steady wins the race" mentality.

So when I decided to change course with holidays many years ago, it was a little overwhelming, which kept me from doing anything. Actually, Pinterest kept me from doing anything because they had one million suggestions about everything. It took one search of the word *Advent* on Pinterest for me to quickly resolve to keeping things just as they had always been. And on that Christmas Eve, as I stood there with so many regrets, I knew I missed what was best because I stayed in ignorance, giving in to all-things overwhelming.

Let's not waste another year because these first steps seem too hard.

The very best thing you can do is "baby step" this process. I recommend that you choose one to three things each year and implement that. Get a strong foundation around that tradition and see how it works for you, then the next year implement the following thing. We will walk together through each of the holidays; plus you will create additional references to use for years to come. So all those awesome ideas you hear from others or see on Pinterest, if it inspires without making you crazy, you can jot those down in this book.

Doesn't that sound like a relief? Pressure is off, my friend.

Except there are a few of you who are stubborn and want all the change now. I get it; remember, I'm a fellow extremist. For any woman who has ever gone on a diet (which is most all of us), we know this—you can't lose all the weight on the first day. You can't even lose all the weight in the first month. Those who do lose weight quickly, typically gain most, all, or more back just as quickly because nothing really changed. Those who keep it off are the ones who slowly learned how to change their habits. We are also doing slow, committed change. I know that's not at all what you want to hear, but I wanted to lay all the cards on the table now. We can imagine that by the time we've turned the last page of this book that everything will be better. That we will have magically transformed holidays. I want to say I wish that was true, but I won't. The work is the refining part and it's the beautiful part of the journey too . . . even if it just so happens to be the most annoying part.

When I started working toward losing weight with my nutritionist, Amber, do you know how we started? That's right, one baby step at a time. Week one my goal was to start eating breakfast. I mean, how silly is that? I'm a grown woman—it should be assumed that I can handle eating breakfast. It shouldn't have to be an assignment that includes talking to a nutritionist for an hour and taking an entire week to work on. That is shame, and we already addressed shameful thoughts. So for a week I focused on breakfast. We made a list of three go-to healthy breakfast options. I committed to eat before my kids woke up, since that was one of my issues was not eating until all kids were up, taken care off, off to school, or down for naps. I put myself last and forgot about the basics. Shame kept me from realizing this. Do you know what week two homework was? To start my day with hot tea, instead of three cups of coffee. Ugh, I know. I almost stopped this whole thing. We talked through the benefits of starting your day with hot tea first. So I do that now; I start my day with hot tea, then breakfast, and then I have coffee. She knows that coffee is one of the great loves of my life and that wasn't something I was going to give up, so we kept it. Each week we continued doing one thing and because of that, I'm still doing it all these months later. This hasn't been an extreme change, but a gradual one.

This, my sweet friend, is what I want you to consider doing. It will feel painfully slow at first. However, in five years, ten years, and decades from now when you've reset your entire holiday culture for yourself, your family, and, likely, much of your community, you will be glad you took baby steps instead of sprinted and quit.

Just like my nutritionist let me keep the things I loved, like coffee, I want you to do the same—keep the parts you love, take out the parts that aren't healthy, and add in the things that would make it a "better way." Making holidays more sacred doesn't mean we become one of *those* Christians. You know the type, and we will talk more about them at the end of the book.

FEAR NOT, FOR I HAVE

To close out this chapter, I want you to read Isaiah 43, keeping in mind everything we've discussed: your regrets, His better way, and the baby steps you are about to take. This chapter in the Bible is one of the most life-giving chapters for me and I hope it wildly encourages you. Don't skip this part; take the time to slowly read through it.

As you read, ask your Father to heal the regrets, silence the shame of the enemy, show you a better way, give you the courage and faith to take the next baby steps, and for an increased trust that He will lead you and that He is able. I'm going to encourage you often to write in this book to make it the most awesome holiday resource you've ever had.

- Read through this Scripture once and just hear it.
- Then read it again and circle all the references of God (His name or reference to Him in any context).
- Then read it one last time and underline all the actions He has done, is doing, or will do (for example, in verse 1 you would underline the words "created" and "formed").

But now thus says the LORD, he who created you, O Jacob, he who formed you, O Israel: "Fear not, for I have redeemed you; I have called you by name, you are mine. When you pass through the waters, I will be with you; and through the rivers, they shall not overwhelm you; when you walk through fire you shall not be burned, and the flame shall not consume you. For I am the LORD your God, the Holy One of Israel, your Savior. I give Egypt as your ransom, Cush and Seba in exchange for you. Because you are precious in my eyes, and honored, and I love you, I give men in return for you, peoples in exchange for your life. Fear not, for I am with you; I will bring your offspring from the east, and from the west I will gather you. I will say to the north, Give up, and to the south, Do not withhold; bring my sons from afar and my daughters from the end of the earth, everyone who is called by my name, whom I created for my glory, whom I formed and made."

Bring out the people who are blind, yet have eyes, who are deaf, yet have ears! All the nations gather together, and the peoples assemble. Who among them can declare this, and show us the former things? Let them bring their witnesses to prove them right, and let them hear and say, It is true. "You are my witnesses," declares the Lord, "and my servant whom I have chosen, that you may know and believe me and understand that I am he. Before me no god was formed, nor shall there be any after me. I, I am the Lord, and besides me there is no savior. I declared and saved and proclaimed, when there was no strange god among you; and you are my witnesses," declares the Lord, "and I am God. Also henceforth I am he; there is none who can deliver from my hand; I work, and who can turn it back?" Thus says the Lord, your Redeemer, the Holy One of Israel: "For your sake I send to Babylon and bring them all down as fugitives, even the Chaldeans, in the ships in which they rejoice. I am the Lord, your Holy One, the Creator of Israel, your King." Thus says the Lord, who makes a way in the sea, a path in the mighty waters, who brings forth chariot and horse, army and warrior; they lie down, they cannot rise, they are extinguished, quenched like a wick: "Remember not the former things, nor consider the things of old. Behold, I am doing a new thing; now it springs forth, do you not perceive it? I will make a way in the wilderness and rivers in the desert. The wild beasts will honor me, the jackals and the ostriches, for I give water in the wilderness, rivers in the desert, to give drink to my chosen people, the people whom I formed for myself that they might declare my praise." (Isa. 43:1–21)

We silence those whispers of shame over our regrets with truth—His truth. It's simply not about us or our efforts; it's always been about Him. I hope you were in awe as you circled all those references about Him and underlined all He has or will do.

I want to wrap up this chapter by praying over you, my new friend:

Jesus, would You help my sister to believe this is all true of her. Silence, in the name of Jesus, all those lies of the enemy and accusations she hears from the regrets she has over past holidays. Free her from carrying that any longer. Give her a greater determination to change course than she has ever had before. Help her to desire and believe that there is a better way, more than any thought she could dream or way she could plan. You have said, Father, in Isaiah 55 that Your ways are higher. Help her to take the first step to higher, but keep her eyes fixed on You alone.

Lord, thank You for Your Word and all that Isaiah 43 showed us that You are. We proclaim, Father, that You are the creator of my friend, specifically formed by You. You are her redeemer. You have called her by name. By name, Father, You know and speak about her and to her! You call her "Mine"; she is Yours. You see her walking through the waters, and yet You are with her. You see her when she walks through the fire, and You keep her from being burned or consumed by the flames, even if she is surrounded by them. You say You are the Lord her God, the Holy One. You've exchanged so much for her. You see her as precious and honored and You love her. You don't want her to fear when You tell her You are with her, and You are Father—always with her. You speak in every direction and tell them what to give and want to withhold nothing from her. You've called her by name. You've created her for Your glory. You formed and made her just as she is. You call her Your witness. You say she is Your chosen servant all so that she would know and believe and understand that You indeed are Him, her Father. Would You help her to really know and fully believe and truly understand that You are Him! Lord, remind her that there has never been a God before or after You. Help her not to give her attention or belief to other gods or idols. Help her to know that You are the Lord and there is no one or no thing besides You that will ever save her. You are God. Your hand is faithful and

Your faithfulness is unchanging and reliable. You redeem her—taking what was and making it new. You are the Holy One over my friend, her Creator. You, Father, will make a way in the sea of her life, just as You made a way for Moses. You will cut the path for her—allowing all that she needs to pass. Help her not to dwell on former things, the regrets of the past holidays, or to even think about them. You, Lord, are doing something new! It's already starting! Help her to see it, feel it, and believe it! Remind her that You will make a way in her wilderness, all she doesn't yet see. You make rivers in the desert, taking what seems impossible and bringing not a way out but a way to sustain her as she makes her way through. Lord, You want her to praise You—give her the words to tell You and others how awesome You are!

Jesus, as she continues on through this book, would You lead her? Give her the space and determination to read this book and the discipline and courage to live it out. Surround her by community and family who will do this with her—a new way, a better way. In Jesus' name, I ask all these things. Amen!

We love you so much, I hope you've heard that throughout this study. We want, more than anything else, to come alongside you during these chaotic and magical holidays and help you know Christ and love others more!

Chat with you soon!

Love you! Mean it.

BECKY KISER + THE SACRED HOLIDAYS TEAM

Made in the USA
Columbia, SC
28 November 2018